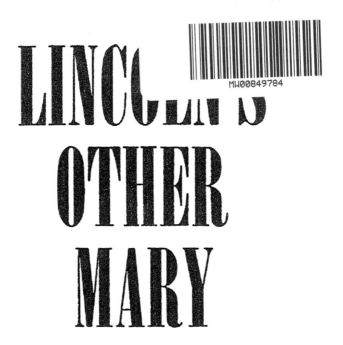

LINCOLN'S OTHER MARY

by

OLIVE CARRUTHERS

Appendix by

R. GERALD McMURTRY

ZIFF-DAVIS PUBLISHING COMPANY
CHICAGO · NEW YORK

BY ZIFF-DAVIS PUBLISHING COMPANY

PRINTED IN THE UNITED STATES OF AMERICA

Acknowledgments

WE WISH TO EXPRESS OUR DEEP INDEBTEDNESS TO THE FOLlowing: Ralph G. Newman, of the Abraham Lincoln Book Shop, who conceived the idea for our collaboration; Dr. Harry E. Pratt, of Beloit, Wisconsin, recent Executive Secretary of the Abraham Lincoln Association; William H. Townsend, Lincoln student and collector, of Lexington, Kentucky; Dr. F. Lauriston Bullard, formerly chief editorial writer for the *Boston Herald;* Paul M. Angle, Director of the Chicago Historical Society; Dr. William E. Baringer, Springfield, Illinois, present Executive Secretary of the Abraham Lincoln Association of Illinois; Carl Sandburg, of Flat Rock, North Carolina; John M. Hamer, Lincoln student and collector, of Chicago, Illinois; Dr. Stewart W. McClelland and Dr. Robert L. Kincaid, President and Vice-President respectively of Lincoln Memorial University, Harrogate, Tennessee, all of whom contributed their time, interest, and judgment; and particularly to Dr. Otto Eisenschiml, of Chicago, without whose constant guidance, criticism, and unfailing faith the book could never have been written.

Lincoln's Other Mary

Chapter One

ALL THROUGH THE BRIGHT, GOLDEN DAYS OF SEPTEMBER, the great plantation of Nathaniel Owens on Little Brush Creek in Kentucky prepared for its fifth birthing.

It was a long time since there had been a birth in the house. The three boys were big fellows now, and Betsey, the least one, was four years old.

The household had planned long and carefully for the event. The house slaves had laid out the fine linen weeks in advance, and cautioned the midwife to take no other calls that last week of the month. One of the field hands had brought in a great, hard lump of rock salt for the mistress to clutch during her labor, and another had sharpened the axe and hid it under her bed, with the bit turned upward, to cut the pain.

In the negro cabins, great prophecies were conjured up for the new child, which was coming like an afterthought to the rest of the family. "The youngest like to be poorly, but 'e always the smartest," they told one another. "If hit a boy, mebbe he be Governor, or a great gemmun an' have a hund'ed slaves, an' sit on de gallery an' drink mint juleps all day long. If hit come a girl, she be a fine lady an' be

1

co'ted by all de gemmuns, an' mebbe have a duel fit for her han'."

At last the blue-eyed baby arrived. It was a girl, with a dusting of dark fuzz on its head that promised dancing curls, and a prediction of beauty in the tiny features. Looking at her, Nathe Owens knew that this child would become peculiarly his own, his personal fulfilment. She would be his special project. She would have every advantage that his wealth could give her, and would be his companion and comfort in his old age.

The darkies were delirious. This girl baby would be their special charge, too, and would grow up to be the most beautiful, the most genteel, the most sought-after young lady in all Kentucky. And they sang incantations and mixed new, strange conjures for the health and happiness of little Mary.

But even the fond negroes could not forsee that one day, in the far away, wild Sangamon country, Mary Owens would walk on the edge of fame; that, for a little while, she would hold greatness in her hands, hers to keep or toss away; that she might, for her own choosing, have the highest position of any lady in the land.

Spring, 1833

The woman wiped the last of the scouring sand from the smooth pine table and rinsed out the cloth. She called inquiringly up toward the loft for one of the boys to come and carry out the dishwater, but no one answered. The young ones must be all out in the field with their father. Well, she reckoned it was a good thing, for the bigger boys were right helpful with the farm work, and the plowing was late this year. It had been a long, hard winter, with snow drifting into the hollows and the corners of the fields long after the crops should have been in.

One thing she missed in this Illinois country—if she missed any part of her childhood life—was the sweet, early Kentucky spring, with golden Easter flowers underfoot in April, and the sunshine so thick and warm it was like melted butter—you wanted to spread it on your cornbread and eat it.

Here, the winter chill lingered into May, and sometimes June, and then suddenly, almost overnight, it was summer, and the wind from the prairie was hot and heavy with the odors of fruition.

Still, Betsey wasn't sorry she'd followed Bennett Abell so far away from her home and all the things she'd known. It seemed like a dream now: her father's far-flung plantation on Little Brush Creek, and the big brick house, two stories high, with room for everybody, room enough even after her mother died and Nathe Owens married again and the second family began to come. Spring in Kentucky, and the darkies singing as they worked in the fields and about the house. Eleven slaves the Squire had had, brought from Virginia after his father died—almost one to a head of his own family—and not a black one of them who did as much work in a day as Betsey did now. But it was all unreal to her, the easy, lazy life, and the smell of locust blossoms, and the clear, thin, crooning voices.

She wasn't sorry she'd come, Elizabeth Owens, daughter of one of the proudest landowners in Green County. She had lost nothing that mattered in leaving her father's home, for she had followed her man blindly, and they had found their own fulfilment in the rich Sangamon basin, in the richer fertility of their love. What if her house was crowded, and her work was hard? She was pleased with her husband, and their children were strong and healthy—the boys handsome, the girls pretty and well-mannered. And there was a whole untrampled empire here, waiting to be mastered.

Betsey Abell was content. The hardest years of their pioneering were over. They'd made their mistakes—like building their first house on top of the hill where it got all the angry gale from the prairie, and trying to raise tobacco in the over-rich Sangamon loam. Now they were beginning to reap the good seed they had sown.

Only, whenever she went to the door, as she did now to toss out the dishwater, Betsey looked for a long moment to the east, toward the high, ragged bluff that blocked off the river, as though to draw strength from the hill. Higher, rougher than the rounded knobs of Kentucky, it was still the only thing here in Illinois that could remind her of home. . . . .

Glancing now, from long habit, toward the bluff, she saw that there was a creeping shadow of green edging over its thrusting height. Spring was really coming!

Her heart quickened, and started a song. Flowers again in the dooryard; sunshine on the floor; fresh, sweet straw for the bed ticks; the hard slap of the children's bare feet on the sandy clearing; and long, lush evenings when, the day's work done and the young ones asleep, she and her man were tired with the delicious langour of toil, but still not too tired for love. . . . .

It was a long way back to Little Brush Creek in Kentucky. Pioneering had taken a great deal out of her. She was no longer beautiful. The heavy work and lack of comfort and repeated child-bearing had coarsened her figure, roughened her hands, put lines in her face. There wasn't time for making pretty curls or pretty dresses. She and Bennett had grown close to the earth that gave them their substance. Close to the sun and the wind and the driving gales. Close to the stars.

They could have stayed in Kentucky, and they could have lived easily there. Sooner or later, perhaps even now, they could have had a house like her father's, a colored servant or two, racing horses in the stable. They could have had the graceful living that is spelled with mint juleps and light conversation, and fox hunts by moonlight. And they never would have known each other. She would have been occupied with ladies' tea parties, children's dancing lessons, continued obeisance to her father. And eventually, Bennett would have taken to wandering down to the negro cabins along the river on the nights of spring days like this, as all the other young gentlemen did. She would have had half as many children, and a closet full of clothes, and a heart that was never free of pain. . . . . Here, they had discovered essentials, and had become elemental as rain, one in each other.

It was a long way back to Green County, Kentucky, and Betsey Abell was glad of the distance.

Once in a while, she was lonely. Bennett worked all day

about the farm, the children took care of themselves, and she grew hungry for the easy come-and-go of neighbors, for light talk and laughter. Their old friends, the Nances— neighbors and schoolmates at home—were here, as well as the Grahams, who were kinfolk on her mother's side; she and Bennett could count every one in the village their friends. But it took time to go visiting. The distances were greater, and the work of house and farm wouldn't wait while you went gallivanting. Her days, crowded as they were with a thousand tasks, were still lonely.

She turned now and looked down the long road toward the village a mile and a half away. Friends and strangers, peddlers and preachers, came by that road, and they always found the Abell latchstring out, in the Kentucky way.

There was some one coming now, and there was only one man she knew who was so tall, or who loped along with such loose-jointed, awkward easiness.

Betsey hurried out toward the lilac bushes that grew in a circle with a hollow in the center, where the little girls were playing house.

"Nancy! Mary!" she called. "Go fetch your father from the north field!"

For Abe Lincoln was coming to call, to sit a spell with his friends, and talk over the latest news of the village.

Betsey surveyed her family crowded about the long deal table, and felt that she could be honestly proud. At the head of the table, Bennett presided with an air of substantial worth that was almost reminiscent of her father. The children's scrubbed faces shone, up and down both sides of the table: the big boys, John and Samuel (Sam named for her brother who had gone pioneering out to Missouri), strapping fellows; Nancy, who was already taking on the mannerisms of a "young lady." Betsey had put Oliver, the little boy, on one side of Abe, and Mary (called after her sister) on the other, so that he could help them with their eating. She kept the baby herself, balancing him against one hip as she moved back and forth from the fire to the table, carrying the food with her one free hand. You learn to be handy waiting on eight people at one time! But this was good, this was living, she thought now: the children washed and hungry, and a friend to share their food.

"It's a right smart thing I knocked that rooster in the head this morning, isn't it, Mama?" bragged John. "I must've had a tremor we were goin' to have company!"

"You're a good boy, John," she replied, with a warning frown. For it was no secret in the family that Betsey was concerned about Abe's sketchy living, and tried to put a real meal on the table whenever he came. She hoped to heaven the young ones wouldn't make any remark about the white-flour biscuits she'd stirred up at the last minute, for white biscuits were a Sunday treat. On week days, she gave them cornbread.

Blessedly, Bennett caught her concern, and began to talk crops. "I'm goin' to have a right good stand of corn in the far field this year, Abe," he remarked in his slow, drawling way, "if the weather's favorable. It's taken me ten years to work up that field to do me any good. Seems as if I never had time to grub out the stumps and get it cultivated right. But the boys pitched in and helped me this spring, and with any luck, I may grow a barrel of whiskey on that field this summer!"

"Bennett," interjected Abe thoughtfully, "I'm goin' to get out of the store."

"Why, Abe?" protested Betsey. For the store, while it didn't give Abe much of a living (he was too honest to make money off his friends), did give him prestige in the village, and he had seemed happy there. Moreover, it was the only place where the women could go to shop. Abe had kept it decent, and a woman could go in without fear of being insulted by drunken loafers. You knew, too, that you'd get your money's worth from Abe, and maybe more.

"Well, I reckon I wasn't cut out to be a business man. Seems like I can't sell enough over the counter to pay for what Berry takes out of the barrel. Anyhow, he's fixin' to get a license to sell whiskey by the drink, and I can't hold with that."

"That'll mean drinkin' all over the place, won't it?" remarked Bennett.

"It'd be mighty hard to stop it," replied Abe.

Bennett frowned. If there was one thing he had hung onto in the years of pioneering, it was his respect and concern for women, nice women like his wife, and the wives of the other men who had settled to make homes in the Sangamon. Betsey had had to do menial tasks that had hurt his pride, and hurt his heart to see her doing, but she had always been treated by every man in the community with the deference that was due a lady. "I don't guess there'll be any store in town fit for you to go into then," he told her now, "you'll have to learn to trust me to get your thread and coffee."

Betsy pushed that thought aside impatiently. There were more important things to consider. "What will you do for a living then, Abe?" she pressed him.

"Oh, I kin always get along," he replied easily. And then, hesitantly lest they think he was bragging, "I'm goin' to get the appointment as postmaster, it looks like."

"Are you sure? When?" Betsey was excited again now. For the office of postmaster carried dignity, and a little bit of glory. It would be a real step up for their friend.

"Well," he said, almost sheepishly, "seems as though the folks got up a petition around town, and sent it to President Jackson. I told 'em not to, because I didn't want any man unseated for my benefit, but they were gettin' a little bit tired of Sam Hill's foolin' around an' neglectin' the mail, like it wasn't much account."

"They were right, too! That's a responsible position, a government position! A man ought to take it seriously!"

"And they told me they were goin' to protest about him, whether I wanted the appointment or not. So I reckon I'll get it. Nigh every man in town signed the petition—exceptin' Jack Kelso, he was off fishin' someplace—and all the ladies."

"There be much of anything in it for you, Abe?" put in the practical Bennett.

"I can't rightly guess. The postmaster takes his pay in commissions. You all better start writin' letters to your folks, so you'll get answers back."

"Will you frank our letters for us, Abe?" bubbled young

Samuel. "We're your best friends. Will you give us Grandfather's letters free, will you?"

"The office of postmaster is a very responsible position, son," replied Abe, with exaggerated gravity. "Tell you what, though: I'll bring your mail out to you, on foot, as soon's it comes in, and you won't have to trek into town after it!"

It was time to hustle the children off to bed. "You'll stop over night, won't you Abe?" Betsey urged him.

Abe slipped his rough brogues off, to give his feet a rest. "Oh, I reckon so, since you mention it. It's a right fur piece back to town."

"That's fine," and Betsey hurried the smaller youngsters up the ladder to the loft so that Abe wouldn't hear Mary's protests. Little Mary liked Abe—he had a way with all children—but she didn't like to have him stay over night, for that meant that he would sleep with the big boys and she would be tucked into the foot of the bed—with three pairs of feet in her face. But there was no other way for Betsey to manage: Nancy was such a big girl that she had to be given the one single bed, and Oliver kicked in his sleep and couldn't be put in with Abe and the others. But Betsey Abell wasn't one to turn a guest out at nightfall, whether the young ones liked it or not!

It took a little time to get them all settled, and when she came down from the loft, the men had gone out into the yard to sit under the oak tree. Betsey lingered to set the food away and put out the candles, and their man-talk drifted in to her.

"Well," she heard Abe say thoughtfully, "chances are the man was guilty. I was purty sure myself that he was. But purty sure and legal proof, Bennett, are two different things. The prosecutor had some fancy witnesses—who hadn't seen anything. Character witnesses, who argued that if a man was caught stealin' a hawg two years ago next Tuesday, why it stands to reason he stole money last winter. And Bennett, according to the Statute, you can't sentence a cat for killin' a bird, unless somebody saw her do it—not even if you catch her with feathers in her whiskers. And then the witness has got to prove he has good eyesight and a reputation for tellin' the truth. But Springfield's a mighty lively town. I rode over with Rowan Herndon, and Rowan says to me, 'Abe,' he says, 'there's plenty men here makin' a livin' with their heads instead of their hands. They aren't grubbin' stumps for a livin'.' I told him, 'Just the same, you don't have to convince a stump—you just grub her out.'"

But Betsey heard him sigh, and she knew the fascination that the courtroom had for him—the drama of oratory, the excitement of matching wits against an opponent, the battle of personalities that might hang a man or free him. And she felt again that premonition she'd had, often before, that Abe was a little different from the rest of them, that his thoughts, hidden behind his casual banter, traveled strange roads, where they couldn't follow. What was it he wanted? What was the restlessness that wouldn't let him set his foot down in one place long enough to make a track? It was more—she hoped—than just the pioneer urge to be going on to some other place, any place but here. It wasn't physical restlessness, wanderlust. It was more as though, no matter what he was doing—clerking in a store, fighting Indians, chopping trees—his mind was somewhere else, dreaming some dream that took him far away from the job he was doing. It was a shame he had lost his run for the legislature a year ago. That might have been the answer, but he hadn't been well enough known in the county, and instead of campaigning to make up for that, he had gone off chasing Black Hawk. No, thought Betsey, it was something else, some longing in him that hadn't yet found enough expression for him to recognize it and do something about it. He was still growing, painfully, like her own boys, who at times had so much energy they didn't know what to do with it, and they wore themselves out chasing each other around the yard, pointlessly. Abe was chasing himself around the yard, without knowing what he was running for, or where. . . . .

She went out to join the men, and their talk at once became casual. She sat down on the ground beside Bennett, and sighed contentedly. "There's goin' to be a moon tonight," she said.

Bennett took one of her calloused hands in his, and she leaned closer to him to see the moon inching up over the top of the bluff. They all three sat silent, and the spring night was like a caress upon their faces. Somewhere over by the river a hoot owl called, and a guinea hen fluttered sleepily in the oak boughs overhead. They could smell the fresh-turned earth of the fields, and the moonlight was almost fit to drink.

"Time for bed, woman," Bennett told Betsey, gently.

Abe got up abruptly, almost brusquely. "I just recalled," he said in a strained voice, "I've got to draw a deed for one of the Clarys in the morning. He's comin' in early. I'd better get along."

And he started out of the yard without tying his shoe laces, and was a good way down the road before they could make startled protest.

"Well, I'll be daggoned," breathed Bennett, "now what did we do wrong? Folks in town say he's been edgy lately, not hardly sociable any more. Walks right away from customers, or closes the store up and goes off wanderin' in the woods for days at a time. Jack Armstrong's right worried about him. They think he's touched in the head."

"I do believe," Betsey replied wonderingly, "that he's jealous of us. Bennett, he ought to have a wife!"

"Oh shucks, Honey, if he needs a woman he knows where to get one!"

"Not that kind!" she protested hotly. "A nice, sensible, decent woman, who'd make a home for him, and care about him, and have children for him! Something he could anchor to!"

"I don't know where he'd find that kind of woman around here," Bennett was serious again, "the good ones are all taken." He put his arm around her and urged her silently toward the house. As always at his touch, her spirit leaped to meet him. But only a part of her responded, for Betsey was thinking. Abe Lincoln needed a wife. . . . .

Chapter Two

*A*BE CLIMBED UP TO HIS BED AT THE RUTLEDGE TAVERN without speaking to anyone. The place was dark, but he didn't light a candle. He took off his shoes, and slipped the single gallus from his shoulder, and sat down on the edge of the bed.

The night air drifted into the room through the solitary window, the same promise-laden spring breeze that had stirred his friends to an emotion that shut him out, and *made him alien and lonely.

God! Would he always be lonely, even when he sought company? There had been times when he was in the midst of a crowd, at a gander pulling or a political meeting, when that sense of aloneness had taken and possessed him until he was afraid to speak to the man next to him, for fear the fellow wouldn't understand his talk. Why should he feel different from the people around him? He came from the same kind of folk as the majority of settlers about New Salem—maybe poorer than most—and he did the same kind of work for a living. They were no more restless than he, with their forever pushing on to fields that looked greener

14

until they got to them. And yet, his was a different kind of restlessness from theirs. For they knew they wanted the next pasture. He didn't know what he wanted. . . . .

Maybe it was an easier way of living. His father had taught him to do physical work, and to do it well, but he had never taught him to like it. Perhaps he wanted to work, like the lawyers he'd seen in Springfield, with his head instead of his hands. Maybe it was the excitement of politics that could feed the hunger that food didn't help. It might be that.

It might be a woman. . . . .

Not just any woman. But one who could understand him better than he did himself, and who could love him for what he was even while she tried to help him to be something different. . . . .

A woman who could love him. . . . .

Would any woman flame to his touch as Betsey had tonight for Abell—after more than ten years with the man?

Was it a woman he needed? Was it only a woman?

Two women hadn't stayed the restlessness in Tom Lincoln. Could one do any more for his son?

Just the other day, Hannah Armstrong—Jack's wife—had told him it was time he settled down. "It wouldn't matter so much to you what you did for a living, or how hard you worked, if you had a good girl waiting for you at home, Abe," she had said. "You'd have something to tie to, something to work for."

Something to work for. Something besides himself; a self that, after all, wasn't very important. And yet, an anchor could weight a man, hold him down, clip his wings, and keep him earth-bound forever.

But his thoughts kept circling back to the man and wife he had just left, the woman who had given up ease and luxury to go pioneering with her mate, who had learned a whole new way of living and had borne him six children, and still went breathless at his touch. . . . .

Abe got up from the bed and lit the home-made candle. He carried it over to the streaky mirror above the wash stand, and looked long and searchingly at his reflection in the glass.

Then with a sigh, he put out the light, and stretched his long length on the bed. He wouldn't sleep much tonight. For what woman that he would ever want could be expected to take him?

Chapter Three

At LAST THE BIG HOUSE WAS QUIET. THE TWO YOUNG ladies, perfumed and giggling, had gone off with their beaus, and Mary's stepmother was upstairs hearing the children's prayers. Nathe Owens had retreated to the gun room, which he used for a study.

Mary started to follow him, to tell him of the letter she'd received from Betsey that morning. She knew he was curious, for he had brought it in from town himself, and it was one of the few from Illinois addressed specially to Mary. Most of Betsey's letters were written to their father, but meant for the whole family. Nathe hadn't asked to see the letter, but Mary knew that he expected her to tell him, for she had never kept anything from him.

Yet, this was something that she didn't want to share with him. She would have to tell him, sketchily, what Betsey had written, but she couldn't show him the letter.

For Betsey had said: "If you got away from Papa for a little while, you might find that things look very different to you. There are a lot of fine people here, who will make their mark in the world. Not many of them went to dancing school when they were young, but they are all good stock—

our kind of folks, from Kentucky and Tennessee and the Carolinas—and we're building a new nation out here, just as surely as Papa helped build Kentucky. But it's been a long time since Papa had only a wagon and a team to his name, and he's forgotten that women were ever anything but ornaments. We have one friend in particular . . . . he's just been appointed Postmaster at New Salem, and Bennett and I think he will go far. . . . ."

Betsey went on to urge Mary to come to visit her in Illinois. She had seen none of her kinfolk since she left Kentucky over ten years ago, and though she was very happy, and their neighbors the Nances, and the Graham cousins were almost like one family, still she'd like to see her only true whole sister.

But of course Mary couldn't go. A long, dangerous journey like that, unattended—why, it was only a year ago Betsey had written that all the young men had gone off to fight Indians! And all the houses were built of logs, and the streets of the town nothing but mudholes, and the mail came only twice a week. Mary had never been able to understand how Betsey, her own blood, had been able to go off to the wilderness to live, so far from everything that she had ever known or been taught to value.

Still—perhaps it wasn't so bad. There was a Baptist minister in New Salem, a Mr. Camron from Georgia, who ran a grist and sawmill during the week and preached on Sunday in the schoolhouse. There were two doctors, though Betsey had written that Dr. Regnier was drinking himself to death. The other one, a Dr. Allen, was a violent Prohibitionist, so maybe that evened things up. Anyhow, Betsey had had her babies quite successfully, and from all reports, they were healthy youngsters.

She'd never seen one of Betsey's children. Six of them, there were now. Where had the years gone since Betsey went away?

For Mary, they had been filled with an endless and not unenjoyable minutiae of small tasks and small events—helping to bring up the children of her father's second marriage, who had come along as rapidly as his first family; sharing the management of the house and servants with her stepmother; church, books, occasional shopping and business trips with her father to Bardstown and Louisville and Elizabethtown; long talks with her father who, in spite of his remarriage, seemed to look to the last child of his first love for his real companionship; weddings and births and sicknesses and deaths in the negro cabins.

Lately, Mary had found an enlivening interest outside the circumscribed orbit of her duties: the growing temperance movement. There was evidence aplenty of the evils of drink near at hand, among the small farmers in the knoblands who nearly all had their own "stills" for making whiskey; over in Nelson County where the distilleries were large and well built; and among the darkies in the neighborhood and on their own plantation. Squire Owens had got mighty worked up over the situation, and, harking back to the time when he had been a high sheriff, argued that the problem was entirely one of enforcing the law, and talked about how much better things were handled in the old days. But Mary was inclined to agree with a song that was becoming popular among temperance advocates, that went, "a man can get

drunk in a licensed saloon just as well as in one that's free."
The question was one of education toward self-control, she
argued with the Squire, and he listened respectfully, as
though she were another man, but he was never convinced.

Mary found a great deal of satisfaction in working for the
temperance cause. But it was cold comfort, and she knew
quite well that it was a small substitute for the normal life
that every woman has a right to expect.

And while the years had slipped unobtrusively away until
Mary was twenty-five and young no longer, Betsey had been
living fully, strenuously. Betsey had known both the hardship and the excitement of going to a new country with the
man she loved, and of working shoulder to shoulder with
him for their good and that of their children. Betsey had
known the deep fires of a man's love, and the recurring
glory of motherhood.

Betsey's life had been real, alive, and pulsing, while Mary's
had been filled, like a schoolgirl's, with time-killing pre-
tenses. . . . .

Mary knew that she shouldn't be discontented, when Papa
was so kind to her, giving her everything she wanted. She
had had the privilege of book learning far beyond that of
most women of her time, and she had a beautiful home, fine
clothes, a definite social position as Squire Owens' "smart"
daughter. She was loved and respected by her father, his
wife, their children, and the servants.

But she felt the futility of her life again and again, especially at night when, the daily tasks done—and her young
half-sisters, aged seventeen and fifteen, were out cavorting
about the county with their beaus—she lay in bed wonder-

ing what was in store for her, what might happen tomorrow. But tomorrow always turned out just like today, not unpleasant, not exciting, just the same.

She had a good and well-trained mind, and she had been told that she was beautiful. But nothing had come of her looks and her education except her companionship with her father, her position in his household as a sort of second hostess. She loved her four half-sisters and half-brother, but they were not her own children. What would become of her if Papa died—when he died? Bereft of her one congeniality, an extra female in this house or the home of one of her sisters or brothers, with no intimates and no rightful place of her own—an old maid? Sometimes, in her troubled nightly questions, she reached out a hand in the dark and touched the smooth, uncreased pillow next to hers, half caressingly, not knowing why she did it. . . . .

She had had beaus. But it seemed that nearly all the really promising young men had gone away to Illinois, or Indiana, or Missouri. Some restlessness had taken hold of them in the unsettled decade after the war with England, and they had gone hunting moonstones, like Betsey and Bennett. By the time she was fifteen or sixteen, there were precious few left that a girl with her upbringing could be interested in. And there was something about every boy who'd ever courted her that Papa didn't like. One drank too much, and another was reckless with horses, and another gambled. Still another found the negro cabins too attractive.

Now Mary was twenty-five, and mature beyond those years from constant companionship with her father. And it was certain that before long, that young Vineyard boy who came to see her half-sister Nancy every night, would be speaking to Papa. Even Ellen, only fifteen, was such an outrageous flirt that she didn't show promise of remaining single much longer than Nancy. . . . .

Betsey had written, "If you got away from Papa. . . . ."

There were strong men in the West, in the Sangamon country. Betsey had said so. And they were lonely men, for there weren't many women there. Perhaps a woman's age wouldn't matter so much. . . . .

"I'll go," Mary promised herself. "I'll get around Papa some way. I have a right to visit my only true sister. And besides, there may be temperance work to do there."

So, her conscience quieted, she went off to find the Squire.

Chapter Four

$\mathcal{A}$BE LINCOLN SAT UNDER A TREE IN THE YARD OF SAM Hill's store, trying to figure out some way to lick the August heat that rose like steam from the prairie. He removed one brogan, then the other, and rubbed his feet against the grass. But the grass was parched and dry, and hot to his touch. He sighed, fanning himself with his old straw hat, and looked again at the paper in his hand.

He knew well enough what it said. It was a summons to appear in the Sangamon Circuit Court—along with Dave Rutledge and William Greene (young William)—on the bond they'd executed to Alexander and Martin Trent in January, "to secure the conveyance of the east half of Lot number five South of Main Street in the first survey of the town of New Salem." The bond was for a hundred fifty dollars, but as far as Abe was concerned, it could have been for a hundred fifty thousand. He'd be just as likely to get hold of one sum as the other.

That wasn't the only court action that was staring him in the face, either. Only a week ago, he'd been served with a similar paper by Sheriff Henry, who'd got tired of waiting for Captain Bogue, of the unhappy little wood-fed steamer "Talisman," to return and pay up the note that Abe and Nelson Alley, in a great flush of friendliness, had signed better than a year ago when it looked as if the captain would surely open up traffic on the river. It had seemed safe enough at the time. If a man is your friend, and appears honest, why, you sign his note just as you'd recommend him for membership in the church. Nobody around New Salem had much of any collateral. A man borrowed on his character, his face—and hope. So when Bogue had asked Abe and Alley to go his paper, and had said he'd sure take care of it, they had taken it for granted that he would. Then Bogue had disappeared, and now Henry wanted the money.

Well, it was a funny thing, mused Abe. The Trents and Henry were within their legal rights. Abe and Alley had signed the note, and they rightfully owed the money in the absence of Bogue. And yet, suing on a note that was executed in friendship was something Abe Lincoln couldn't have done. He'd have taken his loss and forgotten about it.

However, a man can't forget his debts. These obligations of Abe's were honest, and they'd have to be met. His name might not mean much—yet—in the world of men, but people were beginning to call him Honest Abe, and he could think of worse handles to a name. Just the same, paying those debts called for hard cash money, beyond his few personal wants. And where it would come from, Abe had no idea at all.

Sitting there in the hot shade, faced with two lawsuits, Abe tried to figure out what was wrong with him. Over-optimism? He didn't think so. At least, he was no more optimistic than anyone else here in the Sangamon, where opportunity seemed to be lying around like gold in the streets, just waiting for somebody to pick it up. Was his trouble poor judgment? He had a sneaking notion that was it. He should have known, for instance, that he wasn't cut out to be a businessman. The store had looked like a good idea, just as signing those notes had looked like a good idea. A storekeeper is a man of importance in a small community, and is respected. The picture of himself as a merchant was very attractive. And everyone in New Salem liked him, and was anxious to trade with him. When he started in the store, it had just seemed like he couldn't lose.

But somehow, he couldn't haggle over a penny, or weigh coffee or sugar down to the quarter-ounce, or refuse credit where he knew there was need but no money or hope of it. Abe realized too, that it takes application to run any business, and that if a merchant is to be successful, he must plan ahead, reckon probable sales, and buy cannily with an eye to profit and turnover. He understood that the smartest buying and the shrewdest selling wouldn't avail much unless a man kept careful track of inventory and income and outgo. But it seemed like whenever he started to make plans for the store, or to work on the records, somebody came in, and he just couldn't keep from passing the time of day. Then, before he knew it, the afternoon had been talked away, with nothing accomplished but the keeping of a friend.

Moreover, last winter Jack Kelso had helped Abe discover poetry, and he had become acquainted with the sound of words that rippled like running water, or stood out stark and shocking as a leafless tree in the moonlight. He read:

> Full many a glorious morning have I seen
> Flatter the mountain tops with sovereign eye,
> Kissing with golden face the meadows green,
> Gilding pale streams with heavenly alchemy,

and the crude log cabin that housed his merchandise fell away from him, and he was alone and shaken before the sight of pure beauty, so perfect that it squeezed his heart and took the breath from his throat.

He read:

> But, Mousie, thou art no thy lane,
> In proving forsight may be vain:
> The best laid plans of mice an' men
> Gang aft a-gley,
> An' lea'e us nought but grief an' pain
> For promis'd joy,

and he thought that Robert Burns must have known life as he, Abe, had found it, with more disappointments than reward for his hard work, and the sincerest charts and intentions leading him off on by-roads that ended in quagmires of futility.

When he went back to Shakespeare, he found, as though it had been written just for him:

> When to the Sessions of sweet silent thought
> I summon up remembrance of things past,
> I sigh the lack of many a thing I sought,
> And with old woes new wail my dear time's waste—

That was Abe Lincoln all right, in the flesh. Where were

the things he sought? How had they eluded him? What was he seeking, anyhow?

Well, he didn't wail the loss of the store. It was better to realize now than later that he wasn't a tradesman. He'd let go his interest in the same way he got it, by a transfer of paper. To those same Trent brothers who were suing him now. And even if there was no profit in the transfer, there was no loss, either.

The postmastership, coming along so soon after he'd let the store go, had appeared to be a godsend. Manna from heaven, like the story in the Old Testament. But he knew already that its benefits were less material than personal. There were all the papers coming in by the week, to various subscribers—the *Louisville Journal,* the *Sangamo Journal,* the *National Intelligencer* from Washington, and the *Missouri Republican,* and he could read them as he delivered them, and know what was going on all over the country. The uproar over the South Carolina Ordinance of Nullification had hardly died down, and the papers were still discussing the pros and cons of the Tariff Acts which had led up to the Ordinance. The journals had published letters and opinions on both sides and the President's proclamation in full. Abe was no Jackson man, but the President's speech struck him as mighty fine. The mixed loyalties of the Illinois settlers and the lack of local events kept the arguments alive among them long after the question was actually settled. The speeches and arguments excited Abe, and he studied them carefully, pouncing on a tactical blunder here, an illogical assumption there. He became one of the best-informed men in the county on political events.

The postmastership kept Abe close to the people. Folks whom he might not see in a month of Sundays if he didn't deliver their mail to them.

But there was very little money in the job. With his remuneration dependent on commissions, he couldn't hope to make more than seventy-five or eighty dollars in a year's time.

Well, a man could live. He could eat and sleep by picking up odd jobs from the farmers, clerking in Hill's store—where he was keeping the post-office—or helping out at the mill.

He could live, but he couldn't pay any debts that way. Money. Hard cash money to pay off those ill-begotten notes. Now, immediately, he would have to find some way, within the limits of whatever abilities or handicaps he had, to earn more than a living.

But what? If there were only some one he could talk to about it. Some one whose vision was long, who could help him see into the future, who could understand and even aid him in crystallizing his half-formed dreams. Some one who could realize that, without conceit, he felt there was a different plan for him than for the others in New Salem, dear friends though they were. He almost needed, he told himself wryly, some one who could make up his mind for him. . . . .

Betsey? Betsey Abell, who seemed at times to catch some inkling of his hopes, his vague ambitions? Betsey could understand, and Betsey had ability for something besides baby cleaning. But he shied away from the thought. Betsey was another man's woman, whose first thoughts were possessed elsewhere. . . . .

Jing, but it was hot! If the farmers didn't get rain soon even the corn would burn up in the fields.

A man was approaching the store yard, slowly, hesitantly.

"Howdy," Abe offered casually. "When you reckon we're due for rain?"

"I dunno," the other replied, "but Abe, my wife's ailin' again. She's expectin' a letter from 'er mother, sayin' whether she kin come out here to take care of 'Liza an' the younguns, and when she's comin' and all. But we bin mighty hard up this summer—"

Abe got the implication without forcing the plea any farther. "I think there's a letter in there for her now," he said, "bin layin' around a couple days till you come in or I should have call to go out your way." Then he turned, and pointed over toward the bluff. "Looks like a rain cloud caught on the hill, don't it?" he remarked. Then, "Reckon I owe yore wife plenty for free meals an' such. Take yore letter an' fergit it."

After the man had gone, Abe sighed. It wasn't much to do for a friend, but that was the way all his money seemed to go.

Chapter Five

THE WOMEN IN THE NEXT BED HAD QUIETED DOWN AT LAST, and Mary closed her eyes and tried to relax. She was fortunate to have got a single cot in the women's dormitory at the Inn. If she'd had to share a bed with some strange woman—she shuddered at the thought, and wondered whatever had lured her away from her father's home.

Those awful women! Talking half the night away about their confinements, each one trying to outdo the other in sordid and vulgar details. They had glanced slyly at her as they talked, knowing as women will, that they were speaking of experiences she hadn't shared. And when they saw her distaste for their conversation, they had gone gleefully on into intimate stories of their husbands, using words that she had never heard before, the meaning of which she could only conjecture. Well, she'd put them in their places, she hoped, when she rang for the chambermaid to clean the bowl after they'd used it, before she washed her face. And she'd waited until they put out the light, and had undressed in the dark, though she'd flirted for a moment with the idea of making them jealous of her fine, hand-tucked petticoats, made of real imported Irish linen. But she thought

30

better of that, for she couldn't expose herself to these common women who discussed the most private phases of their lives as though they were comparing recipes for spoon bread.

Lying sleepless on the hard cot, Mary's thoughts wandered back over the long day's travel—the tiresome jogging of the stagecoach, the fussing of a tired child, the taste of the cold fried chicken she'd brought along, the smell of the whiskey salesman's cigar, and the singing of the colored coachman. She was alone, among strangers, for the first time in her life.

It had seemed a simple thing to undertake this long journey, but now she was frightened and bewildered, partly by her surroundings, but mostly by the realization of what she was really doing. She had quarreled all summer with her father to get this trip, and she never would have persuaded him without the intercession of Miss Mary Ann, her stepmother. The two of them had always been friends, and had never clashed, though Mary wondered at times how the Squire's wife could endure his deep attachment to the youngest child of his first marriage. Mary had been a little surprised at Miss Mary Ann's aid, nevertheless, and suspected that her stepmother guessed her hope in visiting Betsey, and wanted to help. For Nancy's marriage, just ten days ago, to that Vineyard boy, had been searingly embarrassing for Mary. She wanted little Nancy to be happy, and she had gladly postponed her trip until after the wedding, to help out with the extra work, but after all—

And Nancy's marriage had made Mary all the more determined to go to Illinois, to do something, anything, to change the narcotic routine of her life. So now, in October, Mary was on her way to New Salem, with a trunk full of clothes, a carton of food—Squire Owens had been sure that the food at the inns along the way wouldn't be fit for a white woman to eat, and it wasn't—and his last injunction, "Don't take up with strangers on the way, daughter. Remember you're a lady."

As though she'd ever been allowed to forget it! she mused ruefully. She'd speculated often as to what it would be like, just occasionally, not to be a lady "born and bred," and to be able to do as she pleased, unhampered by the shackles and obligations of her birth and upbringing. What a relief she might find in shouting at some obstinate darky, or in slapping the face of that woman from across the creek who tried to run all the church affairs! But Nathaniel Owens' daughter couldn't do those things. There was precious little that his daughter could do, though of course Papa was right. Good fortune in family and training imposed responsibility, an attitude of noblesse oblige toward all those less happily situated, until women like Mary spent their whole days being polite and gracious, and wondering what they were missing from life.

Well, there was one thing Nathe Owens' daughter could do, and was doing. She could go to visit her sister in Illinois. And this visit to Betsey might easily become an adventure that would break up the pleasant, dull pattern of her living, and bring her happiness of a different quality from the calm contentment she had known.

But now that she was actually embarked upon her adventure, she was beset with doubt. What would the wilderness really be like? Would Illinois be like this wide, unbroken plain of Indiana, with never a hill or a hollow to relieve the

sight or tease the imagination? Betsey had written that the
Sangamon country was beautiful, but Betsey had seen it first
through the eyes of her lover, and it might not look the same
to one who came alone.

How did people live on the frontier? Were there good
shops? Were there any servants available at all? Betsey had
never had any. What did one do for reading so far away
from any cultural center? What kind of house did Betsey
live in, and how could she manage her swarming brood in
such close quarters?

And if Mary should find romance in the West, how could
she bear to leave the younger children of her father's second
marriage? Sarah, only seven, was still almost a baby, and she
had clung to Mary and cried heartbrokenly when she said
goodbye. John, turning twelve, was a handsome lad, serious,
studious as her own brothers had never been. Margarite, in
between the two, was becoming a bit wilful, something like
Mary herself. No one but Mary could really understand her
imperiousness. If Mary should leave for good, what unhappiness might Margarite encounter from want of careful guidance? The older girls wouldn't miss Mary at all. Nancy was
already married, with her own adventure secure, and it
looked as though Ellen would soon follow her example. But
the little ones—it was almost as though they were Mary's
own, for she had helped with their care since they were born,
and they had become part of her. . . . .

Slowly, through the maze of her confused thinking, Mary
came at last to the question which had to be faced, for which
she knew no answer. If she should find romance in the
wilderness—what was marriage? Was it what those two

awful women, now snoring lustily in the bed next to hers, had spoken of so freely? Was it an ordinary, common, animal relationship, with no finesse, no privacy, no restraint? She didn't know. No one had ever told her. Miss Mary Ann had ignored the question entirely, treating her stepdaughter like some neuter companion whose mind was not capable of anything but servant problems. Once, long ago, when Mary had first become conscious of her blossoming maturity, she had asked one of the darkies. But the answer had been only, "You wait till de right man come along, honey-chile. A good man be kind to you, teach you ever'thing you need to know." Betsey? She couldn't ask Betsey, either. She had passed the age for asking such questions. But even Nancy, little Nancy with her head as empty as a blown up paper sack, knew now what Mary didn't.

No, she told herself fiercely in the dark, with people of taste and upbringing, marriage couldn't be what those two women had talked about. It must be a dignified, beautiful thing, based on mutual respect and courtesy; a mental relationship as deep and satisfying as that between herself and her father, with love besides. . . . .

She slept at last, and dreamed of a handsome stranger, clothed in deerskin, who kissed her hands and told her that she was beautiful. But in the morning, when she tried to recapture the dream, she couldn't remember his face. . . . .

Chapter Six

*O*NE MORNING IN OCTOBER, ABE GOT UP, AND KNEW THAT the glooms had left him, at least for a spell. He was a little afraid of those fits of despondency which overtook him periodically without warning and for no known reason, and, while they were on him, made him feel that he was helpless and imprisoned, his work futile, his whole life a mistake. He couldn't understand those black moods. He knew every human being had his ups and downs—Doc Allen, religion-crazy though he was, or Dave Rutledge, or John Camron. Jack Kelso's drinking was an attempt to escape such melancholy; and even the Clary's Grove boys, elemental as they were, had their bad days. Robert Burns and Shakespeare knew moments of doubt, too, if you could judge by their poetry. But he didn't believe any of them got as low in their minds as Abe Lincoln did, and he didn't know how to lick the thing.

You can fight a bear, or an Indian, or a roughneck pioneer, or anything that you can take by the neck and wrestle with. But how do you take hold of a mood to choke the evil breath out of it?

This autumn morning, however, there was nothing to choke. It was a different kind of a day. The sky was as vivid as a bluebird's wing, and the sunshine was like spun gold. You wanted to break off a hunk of it to keep. And there was a tang in the air that stung his senses, whipped a challenge in his face. Why, nothing could throw Abe Lincoln! He was young, he was strong—and not so dumb, either—and it was a big, free country, and he'd get his debts paid somehow. He'd find his way, too, to something bigger, something better than he'd ever dreamed of! It was almost within his reach; he could almost see and touch it. He was as sure of it as he was of tomorrow morning.

He hummed a dance tune off-key—"Bow to your pardner and down the outside"—as he sorted the mail, and he felt so good he just had to do something about it. If he didn't, he'd surely bust!

He found the Louisville paper and a letter for Betsey Abell in the pile of mail, and they gave him a start.

"I haven't seen Betsey and Bennett in a month of Sundays," he thought. "Reckon I better take this out first thing."

The walk out into the country would be fine. It would take care of some of this exuberance that was bursting his insides. And he hadn't eaten any of Betsey's cooking in a long spell, either.

"Why Betsey, that hill looks just like the knobs at home!" It was Mary's first morning at the Abell farm, and she had already spied the bluff. An early frost had turned the oak leaves, and the whole countryside was ablaze with color, like campfires burning, and a blue mist from the river hung over the peak of the bluff like smoke. "It must be a real comfort to you. I became weary of the flat prairies in Indiana, on the way."

They had done their weeping and exclaiming the night before, and now they were ready for a real visit.

"It is a comfort," replied Betsey, setting the baby down on the floor. "I guess I wrote you about our first house. When we came, we were right taken with the view from the high land, so we built up there. It was wonderful—we could sit on top of our hill and look every way, clear out over the country. But when winter came, we like to froze. I don't know how we lived through that first winter, with the snow, and the wind blowin' in off the prairies and not a thing to stop it. As soon as the ground thawed in the spring, Bennett started this house down here in the hollow. Though with the children comin' so fast, it looks like we'll soon outgrow it."

Was there a shade of smugness in her voice? thought Mary. But Betsey looked old, ten years older than Mary instead of the actual four. Her figure had spread, her hair and hands had coarsened from hard work and neglect. Her speech was careless. "You'd never know we'd been brought up in the same house, in the same way," Mary told herself. And yet, there was something in Betsey's face that Mary couldn't find in her own: contentment, and strength that was more than will power, and a look that suggested deep burning fires, only lightly banked. Betsey was happy as Mary had never been!

On an impulse, Mary picked the baby up from the floor where he was playing with some empty spools strung on a cord. He was warm and soft and unexpectedly heavy in her arms.

"I haven't held a baby since Sarah was little," she remarked, as though her act needed explanation.

"He'll ruin your clothes," protested Betsey, but she couldn't keep the pride from her voice. "He's my best baby, though. Never a bit of trouble, beyond what you'd expect from a young one. I kind of hate. . . . ." But no, she wouldn't tell Mary that before spring, Brooks would no longer be the baby. Not yet. Not until they were better acquainted after their ten years apart. She changed the subject quickly. "That's a mighty fancy dress you're wearing, Mary. Didn't you know you were coming to the back woods? You know, once in a long time, I get homesick rememberin' how things were at home. How we used to dress up every afternoon, and have tea in the livin' room. And the firecrackers and eggnogs at Christmas. They don't drink eggnogs here— they just drink whiskey. And they don't wait for holidays to do it either. Thank goodness, Bennett's never taken up with the rounders in town, their drinkin' and wrestlin' and cock fights every Saturday night. I've got a good man, Mary. What's this Vineyard boy like? Do you think Nancy will be happy?" Nancy had been just a little girl when Betsey went away. It was hard to believe that the child was married, settling down to maturity and responsibility.

"I don't know," replied Mary indifferently. "I never saw much of him. He comes from a good family."

Betsey smiled secretly, for she knew by Mary's tone that her sister was jealous, and that she was ready to think definitely about marriage for herself.

"I wish you'd let me do something with your hair while I'm here," Mary went on, still on the defensive.

But before Betsey could answer, little Mary danced in from the yard where she'd been playing.

"He's comin', Mama! He's comin' up the road now! You said he'd come back when he got good an' ready, and here he comes!"

"Who's coming?" demanded Betsey, though she knew quite well.

"Why, Abe! He's bringin' the paper from Lo'ville!" She turned to her aunt. "He makes whistles for the boys," she explained, "an' once he made me a doll out of a stick of wood, but it wasn't much good. He tells us stories about bear hunts an' Indians, and how he got the boat off the dam when it stuck, and revival meetin's in Indianny!" And out she pranced, to meet the guest in the dooryard.

Chapter Seven

"Who is he?" Mary asked, trying to sound casual.

"Well," Betsey felt her way carefully, for Mary had always been difficult to handle, and she wanted to say just the right thing, to whet Mary's interest just enough and not prejudice her against Abe by too much praise, "I wrote you about him. He's our best friend here. He's postmaster in the village, and he isn't much to look at, but he's got a good headpiece on him. Cousin Mentor thinks he'll go a long way before he's through."

She had to stop her recital, for Abe stood in the doorway, stooping to get through, with little Mary tugging at one big hand.

"The mud wagon jist got in," he explained, "so I brought you out your mail first thing." Then he caught sight of Mary, and colored in confusion. He'd heard gossip in the village that Betsey's sister was coming to visit her, but he hadn't known when, and he was unprepared for the splendid stranger in Betsey's living-room. He stammered for a couple of minutes, and then stopped entirely.

Betsey jumped in quickly to fill the gap. Why must the man be so bashful? Yet, it was one of the most appealing things about him, once you got to know him. "This is Mr. Lincoln, my sister Mary. He always delivers our mail first—walks clear out here with it. He had a store in town, too, until last spring," she prattled on, "we were right sorry when you sold the store, Abe. It was the only place in the village fit for a woman to go into."

Abe had taken a chair, and kept little Mary nearby with one long encircling arm, though nothing could have pried her loose. He was too discomfited to glance toward the guest, for he was acutely conscious of his coarse trousers and calico shirt flung open at the throat, and of the dust on his boots from the long walk. He tried to appear at ease by talking to Betsey.

"Well, ma'am, I was mighty sorry to let it go," he replied, "but there can't anybody sell whiskey after it's drunk up, and Berry was drinkin' it 'fore I could git it sold. And then," he knew he'd told Betsey all this before, but he had to say something, "we didn't see eye to eye about sellin' liquor by the drink. You know you womenfolks couldn't go into the store to trade if there was men there drinkin', jist like a saloon."

"I reckon not," admitted Betsey regretfully, "but now you're postmaster, you come to see us instead of our having to go into town to see you. And maybe something else will turn up. How's your case coming?" If she could only keep him talking, Mary would discover what a fine mind he had, and perhaps she wouldn't be so disappointed in his looks.

"Which one?" asked Abe ruefully. "The Trents—we settled up with them, and the case was thrown out."

"And I'll bet you got the worst end of the deal, too!"

stormed Betsey. "You'd give away the shirt from your own back!

"I wanted it settled. I don't like debt."

Betsey didn't know quite what to say next, so she got up and moved the coffee pot closer to the fire. There was nothing like food to foster congeniality! And she knew that Abe was nearly always hungry. "I just made fresh coffee, Abe," she said, "I'll call Bennett in, and we'll all have a cup. Mary, stop hanging on Abe, and go out and play! Abe comes to see us, too, you know. Get Nancy to make you a doll dress!" She shooed the child out the door like a little chicken. "She's goin' to look like you, Mary," she told her sister. She wanted Abe to look at Mary, to see how lovely she was, to see her as a person, as a woman.

When Mary rose to help Betsey with the cups and the fresh-baked bread, Abe did steal a guarded glance at her.

There was no more than the faintest family resemblance between the two, he found. For Mary was a lady, as carefully tended and sheltered as a rare flower. With her elaborately arranged hair, her flounced "morning dress," and her fine soft hands, she was grotesquely out of place in Betsey's crude house. She was tall, and not slim, but she carried herself well, with an assurance that he supposed came from both wealth and training. The two women were talking in undertones, and while he caught only a word now and then, Abe noticed that, in contrast with Betsey's speech, which had become roughened like her hands by her years on the frontier, Mary's enunciation was more careful, her voice better modulated, with a marked Virginian inflection. Her r's were not just forgotten, but became soft "ah" sounds, and when she said "out" it was almost "oot.'

Abe had never seen anything like her before. All the women he had ever known—his mother, Sarah Bush, the wives of the men in and about New Salem—were pioneers' women, primitive, functional females, bent and warped by the stringencies of their lives, having long ago forgotten any niceties or amenities of living they had ever learned. Mary Owens was like a princess out of some fairy story, with her curls and her pretty clothes and her pretty manners. She was pure landed southern aristocracy, and compared to her, there wasn't much of the old plantation left in Betsey. Just the same, Betsey was comfortable. A man knew where he stood with her, and what to say to her. What in the world could he find to talk about with her sister?

Strangely enough, he had already said something that interested her, and when Bennett came in and they all sat down to their coffee, Mary spoke to him directly. "Betsey tells me, Mr. Lincoln," she said, "that the temperance movement is getting some foothold here, and that there's sore need of it. Are the crusaders really having any success?"

"Not that you would notice, Miss," he stammered, flustered by her attention, "Doc Allen, he does a lot of temperance talkin', but there seems to be jist about as much drinkin' as ever. I don't hold with it myself—nor chewin' nor cursin' either—but pioneer life ain't easy. The men work mighty hard, and it gits right cold in the winter time."

"Do you think the women could be roused to any enthusiasm?" demanded Mary.

"I couldn't rightly say," he replied earnestly, "they don't

have much time for anything but washin' and cookin' and scrubbin' and takin' care of their babies. Betsey could tell you better."

This temperance talk bewildered him. Miss Owens was so obviously a gentlewoman, you wouldn't expect her to have a thought in her head except of beaus and doodads. Then he recalled that this was Betsey's "educated" sister, who had gone to a convent school, and whom their father had raised to be a mental companion to him. This recollection confused him more than her looks and her manner, and Abe suddenly made an excuse to get back to town. There was the rest of the mail to be delivered.

"I'll come to see you again, if you don't mind," he floundered, and got out of the house somehow.

Bennett went with him as far as the road, and came back chuckling.

"What's so funny, Bennett Abell?" demanded Betsey. "You act like you'd swallowed the wrong way."

"Oh, Abe told me a funny story. About a preacher and an old maid—I'll tell you some other time," for a quick look at Mary stopped the tale, and he ducked out of the house toward the wood lot.

Abe Lincoln walked slowly back toward the village, his thoughts in a strange confusion.

Chapter Eight

*B*ETSEY HAD FORGOTTEN HOW STRONG-HEADED MARY COULD be. But now, on the third day of her visit, when Mary started talking about going to call on the Nances, Betsey remembered that Mary had pretty nearly always managed to get her own way about things, even when they were children. And the habit had seemed to grow on the younger sister with the years.

It was perfectly natural for Mary to want to see Parthena Nance. For the Nances were neighbors from home, who'd come to Illinois about the same time as Betsey and Bennett. The girls had practically grown up together—Parthena had studied with Betsey and Mary, for Nathe Owens had been eager to share his children's tutor with the neighbors' youngsters. As a matter of fact, Betsey hadn't seen Parthena for several weeks herself, and it would be right nice to take a day off and go visiting.

She didn't want to fuss at Mary during this visit, either. She was anxious to become better acquainted with the sister who had been only a child when she left home, and to get to be real friends with her, as adult kinfolk can be.

But what if Abe Lincoln came to call while they were gone? It wasn't only because of her interest in Abe that Betsey wanted Mary to like him. She was thinking of Mary, too. Of that soft, padded, unreal, sterile life Mary seemed to be condemned to at home, shadowed and imprisoned by her father's domineering, empty of any personal meaning or happiness.

Betsey often wondered, when she thought of her old home in Kentucky, whether living there hadn't degenerated into a question of manners, of doing things in the "proper" way, until the form became more important than the substance. Nearly all the young people she knew had migrated, come west to the frontiers where life was hard, and dangerous, and real, and what a man was and did meant more than the way he did it.

There was a sickness on the South, the illness of the old who cannot accept new ideas, new ways to fit the needs of the day. They tried to force the problems to fit the old manner, the old pattern. Why, if Papa could see her now, Betsey, in a calico house dress, her hair combed but uncurled, her hands rough from dishwater and wash water, he'd think she'd sold her birthright! Perhaps she had, but she had been born again, into a life of essentials, of elemental forces which were as tremendous as life itself, and as compelling. She was living in things as they were, not as a southern gentleman pretended they were.

She didn't envy Mary a whit. For Mary, beautiful, cultivated, well tended, was as meaningless and worthless as the old grandfather's clock at home that had stopped running. The clock was a lovely thing, but it had no use, you couldn't tell time by it. Time had stopped for that clock, and it had stopped for Mary. For ten years, almost, Mary had just gone through the motions of eating, sleeping, making herself pretty, and being polite to people. She had become absorbed into the pattern.

Because they had come away so young, Betsey and Bennett had broken through and out of the pattern. They had grown together, accepting the new ways because they had each other. It would take a shockingly powerful Pygmalion to make a human being out of Mary. Abe Lincoln could be that Pygmalion, Abe whose life had never known any softness, who had, of necessity, been better able at five to distinguish chaff from wheat than Mary could do at twenty-five!

Abe Lincoln could bring reality into Mary's life, and Mary could give him that softness, that graciousness, which he had never had and was hungry for without recognizing his hunger.

If they only would marry.

But here was Mary, two days after Abe's visit, demanding to be taken to the Nances, which would mean a whole day's trip, and Abe, if he were ever to come again of his own volition, would be almost sure to come today! And Abe was as hard to handle as Mary—if he came and found them gone, he'd get discouraged, and think that he wasn't important enough for them to stay home for, and he'd shy away from Mary like a colt caught in the wrong pasture! He had to be teased and led along without his discovering that he was being led. But no, Mary had to go chasing off to the Nances, and make Abe think—if he should come—that she was too good for anyone who didn't come from Green County!

"I don't know why it's so important to go today, Mary," Betsey protested, "it isn't as if you were goin' back home tomorrow. Why, you haven't even been around the farm yet, and Bennett will be right disappointed if you don't show some interest in his place!"

"Betsey," Mary answered patiently, explaining as she would to Sarah at home something the child had never heard of before, "Parthena was my dearest friend, all the time I was growing up. We were like sisters. I knew her even better than I did you, because you were so busy courtin' with Bennett. I want to see her. It's been—lonely—since she left Kentucky."

It was that cry of loneliness that defeated Betsey. Mary had been lonely there at home. She couldn't have been anything else. But good gracious, you can see a girl friend any time, when there are no men around at all!

"Well," she gave in, "we can't start before noon. I'll have to take the three least ones with me, and Bennett can't hitch up the team until he comes in to dinner."

"Oh my goodness, can't you hitch a team yourself?" exploded Mary. "You grew up with horses!"

"Not this kind of horses," replied Betsey dryly, "and not with democrat wagons."—Oh, the riding horses at home! Bennett had promised her a horse of her own, but somehow, they never got money enough ahead for that. Everything had to go back into the farm.—She tried once more to dissuade Mary.

"I should think you'd be much more anxious to see Cousin Mentor than the Nances. After all, he's your own kin." For she was thinking, perhaps Abe would show up at Graham's if he found no one at home here. He was always borrowing books from the schoolmaster.

Mary had an answer for that, too. "Cousin Mentor will be teaching on a week day, won't he? And from all I hear tell, he needs his fees."

Betsey was stopped there, and she knew it. What she didn't know was that Mary was thinking, "Why hasn't he come again? Doesn't he like me? What is he really like, under that shyness? What does he want? What does he think of politics, and religion—and women? And—me? Why doesn't he come again? I can't just sit here, waiting! I have to go somewhere, do something! There's a strange, faraway look in his eyes, as if he were seeing you and still not seeing you at all—what does he see when he looks at a woman, a pretty woman, that way?"

To Betsey she said, trying to sound diffident, "What does Cousin Mentor think of this—this Mr. Lincoln who was here the other day?"

Betsey tried hard to conceal her delight at the turn of Mary's thoughts. "He thinks Abe has a lot of ability, and that he'll go as far as—well, as far as uncontrollable circumstances will allow him. He says there's no limit to Abe's capacity to learn, or to his determination, if he's interested. He says Abe wasn't cut out to work with his hands."

"Was any white man?" asked Mary wonderingly, and then Betsey was exasperated again, as much by Mary's very sincerity as by her lack of knowledge of the hard world. Betsey sighed. For her little sister was about the most difficult person she'd ever known. But it was quite evident that

Mary was interested in Abe, only she didn't want to show it. Perhaps things would work out right after all!

Betsey went out into the yard to catch a chicken, and thought grimly, as she grasped the flopping bird with one hand and a hatchet with the other, "I'd like to see my 'educated' sister do this!"

Abe knew right well Sam Hill's store was no place for the post-office. It was small, and there really wasn't room for two businesses. Moreover, it wasn't his, and his particular friends happened not to be friends of Sam's, so that they didn't linger and visit as they had used to do when he had his own store. And Abe didn't hanker to go chasing around for company; he liked to lie on a store counter, or out under a tree, reading a book, and wait for folks to come along. There was no hope of that here, but he had to have the post-office somewhere. Well, he didn't have to spend much time here unless he was a mind to. There wasn't enough mail coming in to require any amount of clerical work.

The thought of work brought him back again to his never-ceasing problem of sustenance. He really ought to go out to Bowling Green's today and lay up some cord wood. He hadn't promised today particularly, but the Judge had hinted last week that the good days of the autumn were numbered, for the prairie winter set in early.

Still, he didn't want to lay wood today. He wanted to dream. . . . .

It was three days since he had trudged carelessly, unconcernedly out to Bennett Abell's, with no thought in his head except a visit with his friends and maybe a free meal. He'd loitered on the long walk out from the village, thinking dull, prosaic thoughts—wondering, as a matter of fact, if Sarah Armstrong could do anything with his one good shirt that had started splitting up the back—and if Jack Kelso was back yet from his last fishing trip, and whether John Clary had got his corn in before the frost. Dull, bread-and-butter thoughts, not even gingerbread thoughts. And then he had walked into Betsey's house, and had seen—a queen!

That was it. Mary Owens was like a queen, not a princess. For she was too tall, and she was handsome rather than pretty. She wasn't young. But there was something regal about her that was more attractive than fluttering youth. She was a woman, and desirable as a woman. There was no coy pretense about her, though, no flirtatious dramatics. In her speech, she was straightforward and honest, and she didn't bother with small talk.

Yet, she was entirely feminine. It was there in every movement, every gesture, a sort of consciousness, not of social class, but of being precious.

He reckoned that was what went with being a lady—that being sure of herself. He'd never known a lady before.

He wondered if he were afraid of her. "I don't think so," he argued with himself. "She's just different. Women must be pretty much alike, underneath the fancy trappings." But he wasn't sure. Not sure enough to go calling again at the Abell's without an extra pretext. What excuse could he find? There wouldn't be another mail from the south for almost a week. He could say he'd come to help Bennett with the farm work, but he didn't want to work in the field and come in to dinner at the same table with Miss Owens, all soiled and sweating.

There wasn't any local talk of sufficient importance to justify a trip to the country. Now, if there'd been a robbery, or an accident, or even if some neighbor to Bennett had lost a cow, he could walk out with the news.

He sighed. He'd just have to wait until chance offered him a reason. He couldn't bear the thought of appearing presumptuous. He couldn't risk her contempt.

He guessed he might as well go out to Judge Green's and work off his agitation. At least, Nancy might be making gingerbread. "I reckon I like gingerbread better'n anybody," he thought wistfully. "And I get less of it."

Chapter Nine

*M*ARY WROTE LONG LETTERS TO HER FATHER. SHE TOLD him of the Greens, and the Nances whom he had known so well and whose departure from Kentucky had grieved him so, and of the beauty of the country. The wildness must be, she told him, much like that he found in Kentucky when he had migrated from Virginia, although the vegetation was not quite so lush and the flora was a bit different. There were no locust trees, but there was an abundance of elms and maples, turned to flame now after the frost. It was colder here than at home, but the cold seemed drier, and didn't penetrate to the bone.

She told him about Betsey's children, how healthy and handsome they were, that little Mary seemed to be the brightest of the lot, but that she missed the children at home. Of Betsey, she didn't know what to write. For, in spite of her incessant child-bearing—Mary was quite sure there was another on the way, though her sister hadn't told her—and in spite of her endless physical work, harder than any darky could be persuaded to do at home, Betsey seemed happy and contented. Mary couldn't tell the Squire that. For he would be shocked and concerned if he knew the real circumstances of Betsey's living, and he'd want to do something to help, and the Abells were so stiff-necked proud they'd never let him help. Anyhow, Bennett and Betsey were better off than most around here. They had what they wanted—or, perhaps, they wanted what they had.

She knew quite well that was because they had each other, and the children. And she wondered, the ink drying on her pen, whether love and children could make her content in this primitive country, without the things she had taken for granted all her life. She believed that they would. She could adjust, if a man loved her, and if she loved him. . . . .

She turned back to her letter. There was a young man here, she wrote the Squire, in whom Betsey and Cousin Mentor were very much interested. He had had to educate himself, but Cousin Mentor had helped and directed him and believed that he had ability. His people came from Hardin County, but had moved to Indiana when Abraham was quite young. Did Papa remember any Lincolns who lived in Kentucky twenty years ago?

That was all she wanted to say; all she dared to say. For while Mr. Lincoln interested and puzzled her, she had no idea whether he liked her or not, or whether she could like him. But she admired ambition, especially ambition for education, and so did the Squire. Though after the letter had gone, she wondered why she had mentioned Lincoln at all. He was only an acquaintance of her sister's, whom Betsey was fond of and sorry for, who had called once since Mary came, and then because he had mail for the family. It wouldn't be surprising if Mary never saw him again. . . . .

More than a little bewildered, Mary allowed herself to be drawn into the square dance. When Betsey had told her they were coming to a dancing party at Clary's Grove, she had agreed quite eagerly, thinking of the gracious, almost stately parties at home, the good music, the dignified dance patterns, the chivalrous attention that Nathe Owens' daughter always received. Mary liked parties. She liked dressing up and going out. She liked dancing.

But nothing in her experience had prepared her for this party—the boisterous abandonment of fun-starved people who shouted out the changes with the caller, and stamped the accents of the tune until you wondered if the house wouldn't surely fall from sheer vibration like the walls of Jericho. When the call came to "Swing yore podner," the women were lifted clear of the floor, squeezed breathless, and then set down with a thump that left them reeling. They seemed to like it. Nearly all the men had been drinking—and still were, if you could make any guess as to the reason for their frequent trips out the back door—and it wasn't the genteel, mint-fragrant sipping that Mary saw at home, intended for social graciousness, but the kind that aimed, honestly, to get drunk.

As the evening wore on, Bill Watkins, the lone fiddler, and far from sober, sawed his bow faster and faster, challenging the dancers to keep up with the music, until the whirling took on all the hysteria of a negro revival meeting.

Some man whom she didn't know (it was a rule of politeness that a lady guest at a party should dance with every man who asked her) had just set Mary down after a particularly giddy whirl, and, breathless and confused, she looked around for a vacant chair, wondering by what grace she had landed right side up. She found a seat, and tried to restore her curls, which had tumbled out of all decorum, her eyes searching for Betsey and Bennett. What kind of a baby could Betsey expect to have if she jumped around like a kangaroo? Illinois was too far from Green County, too far by a thousand traditions of speech, and manners, and ideas!

Seeking her sister, Mary saw Abe Lincoln, over by the outer door. He stood there, hat in hand, as though he had just come in, and his diffidence and sobriety, even more than his height, set him apart from all the others in the room. He was looking for some one, too, and when he spied Mary, he pushed his way through the crowd to her side.

"You look kind of tuckered, Miss Owens," he greeted her. "Seems as if the light fantastic around here isn't so light as it is fantastic. Mind if I sit a spell with you while you catch your breath?"

Mary smiled ruefully at his frankness [does any woman want to be told that she looks "tuckered"?], but she welcomed the respite from physical exertion.

"You haven't been back to see us," she accused him, with just enough lightness in her tone to make him wonder whether she was serious or not. "Have you been so busy?"

Abe looked at her sharply, but her glance was serene, with no trace of coquetry.

"Well," he fumbled, "I thought you and your sister would have so much going on you wouldn't want to take time to listen to me yarn. And I had a job of work to do for Judge Green."—Did she know any men who worked for a living? Well, Bennett did, even though he didn't "hire out."—

"Would—" he seemed struggling with himself to get the words out, "—would you be free some afternoon, to—to walk through the woods?" He couldn't offer her any other entertainment, but then, fortunately, there wasn't any entertainment to buy in New Salem. Folks had to take their pleasure in one another's company.

"I'd be very happy to," she dimpled, and was sorry for, and still amused by, his instant confusion. He rose abruptly. "Thank you, ma'am. I'll be out right soon. I have to see if I can find Hugh Armstrong now—" and he was gone before he had finished his excuses.

Mary smiled secretly. He was coming to see her, and perhaps she would find out what dreams lurked in those strange grey eyes, and what he saw when he looked straight through you at something beyond. . . . .

Chapter Ten

 $\mathcal{B}$ UT IN SPITE OF HIS PROMISE,—AND HE MUST HAVE GONE out to Clary's Grove that night to see her,—Abe Lincoln did not call on Mary immediately. Once, he came out with the mail when the women were spending the day with Mentor Graham, but he left no message for Mary. And once she and Betsey encountered him in the village, when they went in to shop. He lifted his battered hat gallantly, and inquired after their health and the children, but that was all. He made no mention of a social call, or any excuses, and both Mary and Betsey were bewildered.

Betsey saw all her careful plans going awry, and Mary was piqued by his apparent lack of interest. She wasn't used to being treated indifferently. And to be almost snubbed by a man of so little worldly worth as Abe Lincoln was a little more than she could accept. It was after that fruitless meeting that she began to talk of going home.

And it wasn't only the lack of romance for her in New Salem that hastened her decision, or even the news from her father that Ellen was going to follow her sister and get married at the end of the month to that nice Williams boy whose voice had barely changed. She couldn't get home in time for the wedding anyway, though she realized that, with both of the girls gone, she'd be needed at home to help her stepmother manage the house.

More than these, it was the wildness of the country, the difference of the people. The party at Clary's Grove had brought that difference home to her more forcibly than any other incident of her visit. It was true, as Betsey had said, that all the settlers here were from the South, with no more than one or two exceptions. But not from Mary's kind of South. Or if they were, the hardships of the frontier had robbed them of all graciousness and ease, and left them as elemental as animals. If she had found romance here, she would have been mad to think that she could take root in this alien soil. It wasn't a matter of wealth, or lack of it. Bennett and Betsey were well off, as far as property worth was concerned. It was just that the things Mary had been brought up to consider the necessities of living were unavailable here—they couldn't be transported overland, no matter how much money one had.

Her father's home seemed now like a haven, the epitome of all that was civilized and desirable. Breakfast in bed; a bed shared with no one else, where the room was her own and her thoughts were her own.

A leisurely, ordered day; planning the household activities with Miss Mary Ann; calling on the sick; reading and talking with her father. The hushed voices and deference of the darkies. That was the kind of life to which she had been trained and for which she was suited. Though her occupations at home might be futile compared to building a western empire, they were hers through long habit, and they were pleasant.

Anyhow, Abe Lincoln hadn't come back. . . . .

"I tried to persuade her to stay longer," Betsey told Abe a week after Mary had gone, "but she thought she'd be needed at home, with the second sister getting married. And Papa wanted her back. He's getting old," apologetically, "and he sets a store by her. But she said she'd come back for another visit, as soon as she could."

Betsey didn't tell him that if Mary had wanted to stay, she would have, and that a little more attention from him might have persuaded her. What good would it do to tell him now? For apparently he and Mary just hadn't hit it off, and there was nothing to be done about it.

She did inquire, however, because she wanted to know, "Where have you been the last couple of weeks? We've hardly seen hide or hair of you."

"Well, Betsey," he said, stirring the coffee she poured for him, "I've been scurryin' around robbin' Peter to pay Paul. I finally got something paid off on those two notes to Radford. That's the trouble with doin' business on paper: you buy a business and give a note, then you sell to another fellow who gives you a note, then the other fellow skedaddles and you're saddled with your own note. And the business is gone, and you're paying for a dead horse." He sighed, stared into his now empty coffee cup as though to read his fortune there, and then brightened. "What I really come out to tell you, though, is that John Calhoun is goin' to make me his deputy surveyor. I don't know straight up about surveying, but Mentor Graham thinks I can learn. He's goin' to school me at it. And if I can learn, it may be a way out of my troubles. It's nice work, after you get the know-how."

"Oh, it certainly is!" glowed Betsey with quick sympathy and admiration. "A surveyor is almost a scientist, almost an engineer! Why, George Washington was a surveyor!"

"He was a lot of other things besides that," commented Abe dryly, "but I'm mighty pleased at the chance. I thought for a long time whether I should take it or not. Calhoun's the worst Jackson man in the county, and I can't hold with that. But they told me the job wasn't bribery, and I wouldn't have to support Calhoun's politics if I took it. Somehow, bad as I need a real paying job, I couldn't sell my politics. I may be squeamish and foolish, but that seems more important than bed and board."

"You're absolutely right, Abe!" applauded Betsey. "You see, things are working out for you! With all the land speculation going on, there'll be plenty of surveying to do! I wish," she added thoughtfully, "that Mary had been here to hear about it. Of course, I'll write and tell her, but—"

"I sort of hoped she would be," he replied. "I thought she might be glad to hear."

Betsey studied him intently as he spoke. Then, "She said she'd come back," she told him, though goodness knew when it would be. Just the same, if he were interested, there might be some possibility of persuading Mary—

"You know, Betsey," Abe replied, and the words seemed to form themselves for him, with no volition of his own, "when she comes again, I'm going to catch, tie, and marry that girl!"

Then, surprised by his own boast, he blushed furiously, and fled out the door without even a goodbye.

Chapter Eleven

Spring, 1836

*O*NE SPRING DAY IN THE YEAR 1836, ABE LINCOLN WALKED out to the Abell farm, turning idly in his hands a letter he was taking to Betsey.

The postmark was Greensburg, Kentucky, so the letter must be from one of her family. He wondered if Mary had written it.

Mary Owens. He could hardly remember what she looked like, though he did recall that he'd been mighty taken with her that fall nearly three years ago when she had visited her sister for a brief month. But the memory was so colored with the unhappiness and confusion that had possessed him then that no clear impression of her returned to him now. She was blurred for him into a vision of beauty and a longing for all the things he had never had. A woman, any woman, was only a part of that longing, and a gnawing hunger that he could neither dissemble nor satisfy.

Still, it seemed as he looked back now, that his fortunes had begun to look up after he had met handsome Mary Owens. Perhaps she had brought him luck, or maybe—it was a shocking thought—maybe she had helped him to recognize his ability, and so had unconsciously influenced his slow planning.

For she had told him, and he recalled now better than he could remember her face, the soft, drawling inflection and the earnestness of her voice when she told him, "It is quite possible to study by one's self. It is a little harder than it would be if you were younger and going to school, that's all."

Well, he couldn't say how much he'd learned, but he'd certainly studied that fall and winter. Green as June corn, he'd lit into John Calhoun's surveying books, and he and Mentor Graham had argued away many a night over the knotty, technical problems, wrestling with them as though they were opponents who had to be thrown. They were heavier and trickier than Jack Armstrong—it took more persistence to lick them.

The schoolmaster had taken Abe into his own home to board, so that they could use every spare moment for study— and also, Abe suspected, to keep the would-be surveyor from wasting time talking to everybody who came along in the village. They worked so hard at those stubborn books that when his friends did see Abe, they thought he'd gone into a decline. But he hadn't and finally he mastered the stuff so that in January he got his first assignment as deputy surveyor.

There'd been more glory than money in the surveying, though. Men didn't always have hard cash to pay for such jobs—they were still buying land on paper and on their faces—and oftener than not he'd had to take his pay in goods. The first surveying had been paid for with a buckskin, and Hannah Armstrong had taken it and foxed his pants so that the underbrush would not scratch his legs through the thin cloth. That was mighty fine, but a man can't eat buckskin pants.

So that even with the surveying and the commissions he made as postmaster, he'd still had to depend on menial chores for his actual sustenance. Of course, if he wasn't so all-fired good-natured, he'd have made a little more in commissions on the mail. But shucks, a man had to do a favor for a friend once in a while, and franking an occasional letter wasn't much of a concession.

Yes, that winter of '33 and '34 had been hard, with his debts snarling up worse and worse until he could hardly tell which was which. Every time he got any hard money, there were ten places for it, all equally important, and his financial manipulations boiled down to sleight of hand tricks that amazed even himself.

Then in the spring, with the encouragement of Bowling Green and everybody else in town to justify his own eagerness, he'd run again for the Legislature.

That campaign had been different from his first. There was more party consciousness throughout the county, and the fact that there was no presidential election centered folks' interest on the local contest.

By that time, too, Abe had learned the importance of campaigning, and he had stumped the whole countryside, talking with the farmers, lending a hand with their work, praising the women's cooking (he was generally invited to stop for a meal), and kissing the babies. The babies weren't hard to kiss. Not even the first spring flowers smelled as sweet as a clean baby.—Will I ever hold one of my own in my arms, he thought now, and know that it is a part of me, of my own thought, of my love for a woman? Women. Paradoxical, devious, tantalizing, living their whole lives in some secret world of their own, their bright talk never giving a man an inkling of their real thoughts, so that a man couldn't tell where he stood with them. Would any woman ever love Abe Lincoln?

Well, he'd won that campaign. Nobody now could accuse him of wasting time, frittering away precious days in story-telling around New Salem. Those seemingly lazy days had not been thrown away, for it had been his friends who elected him—Whigs and Democrats alike—though he had declared himself firmly as a Whig, with no ifs and ands about it. His constituency had voted him in because they liked Abe Lincoln, and because they believed in him personally. It was a mighty trust, and he felt keenly his obligation to the folks who had opened this door to him.

Not that I made such a showing that first session, he reflected now. But Vandalia had been a very different kind of place from New Salem. In his own village, he was at ease, he could be natural and unaffected, and know that his friends were his, without strain or attempt to make an impression. He was among strangers at the capital, men from every part of the state, older, most of them, both in age and political experience, polished men who were adept in the ways of society and maneuver.

All Abe could do during that session was listen and try to learn. Listening was fascinating and stimulating to the log-cabin boy: the acts to incorporate banks, turnpikes, bridges, insurance companies, towns, railroads, and female academies. He realized that, taken separately, none of these issues was of any grave importance. But the debate from the floor, the impact of clashing ideas, the interplay of personalities which attended each controversy, were like strong drink to one who had never tasted liquor, and he watched the proceedings patiently, cataloging every phrase, storing every gesture in the back of his mind against the day when he could consider himself prepared to take his place on the floor of the House and make his own personality known and felt.

He'd been appointed to one quiet, unspectacular committee, and had served on some select committees. He was biding his time, waiting, listening.

At the special session called by Governor Duncan in December of '35 he'd made a little more noise. He'd supported actively the measures in favor of the state bank; he'd worked for the passage of acts looking to the construction of the Illinois and Michigan canal, a project in which he was mightily interested since his own bright Sangamon had proved unnavigable; and he'd spoken up for the proposal that Congress allow Illinois to enter not more than five hundred thousand acres of government land on credit in making internal improvements. He was still careful, almost over-deliberate in all his public statements. But in that special session, he had begun to be known and to make friends.

In the meantime, following John Stuart's urging, he'd started studying law seriously. He'd known John in the Black Hawk war, and their friendship had lasted. John, also at Vandalia, as Whig leader in the House, had argued that knowledge of the law would help Abe in politics and would give him a means of livelihood if politics failed him. So Blackstone had filled Abe's evenings at Vandalia and the dry spells between sessions which he spent in New Salem. After the tension and excitement of the Legislature, New Salem seemed to have shrunk and grown shabby, and he missed the quick minds, the sharp mental competition that had kept him alert and keen in the capital city. Besides, now that he felt he had found his direction, he hadn't the inclination to loaf and yarn that he'd had before. So he dug at the law, straining toward the time when he could hang out a shingle—he, Abe Lincoln, backwoods boy from Hardin County, who only five years ago had chopped wood for a living. Abraham Lincoln, attorney-at-law. He had a goal at last, a definite place to work toward.

In the meantime, he'd been re-appointed deputy surveyor under Thomas Neale, who had succeeded Calhoun. He had a lot of irons in the fire now, and life seemed to be trying to compensate him for his early hardship.

Yes, a lot of water had tumbled over Jim Rutledge's dam since Mary Owens had been here. He wondered what the years had given Mary. Had she married? Was she happy? Had she grown old? Somehow, he hoped that time had stood still for her, that life had not touched her or changed her since she had visited Illinois. That she was just the same.

He hurried his stride along toward the Abells, so that he might find out.

Chapter Twelve

*A*NYHOW, BETSEY HADN'T CHANGED. SHE WAS OLDER, ampler of figure—her constant childbearing was exacting its price—and she had acquired, with her husband's increasing prosperity, a dignity that was charming, and faintly reminiscent of her younger and handsomer sister. But the welcome was there, the joy at sight of him that Abe Lincoln had always known, and that had endeared Betsey and Bennett Abell to him almost beyond any other friends he had.

"Abe, it sure is nice to see you!" Betsey greeted him at the door. "Your friends are all so happy over your success," she ran on, "but we do long, now and then, for old times when you came and went almost every day—without the whole state of Illinois on your shoulders!"

"It's little enough I've done for the state of Illinois, so far," he answered seriously as he followed her into the house. "But I hope to do more. It's a heavy responsibility representing my own district, without taking on the rest of the state."

She must hear all about his adventures and small successes at Vandalia, and he told and retold her, and the little splash he'd made at the state capital became a great, shining water-

68

fall as seen through her eyes and from the isolation of New Salem. "I'm beginning to learn my way around," he went on, not wanting to brag, but warmed beyond modesty by her enthusiasm. "Next session I hope to get on some good committees and make myself heard."

"Oh, you will, Abe, you will!" she glowed. "Even those smooth, aged-in-wood old-time politicians are bound to notice you, and recognize your ability!"

"I reckon you got the comparison right, Betsey," he returned dryly. "Next to the born-and-bred politicians I'm as raw as new corn squeezin's." But he smiled. Betsey's faith didn't hurt him any.

"Maybe they need new corn-squeezin's to wake them up," she retorted. "Abe, did you bring us any mail?"

"There, I'd clean forgot it! It's a good thing you remembered. Or is it? If I'd taken your letter back to town, I'd have an excuse to come again tomorrow!"

"Do you need an excuse? Wait while I read it."

He waited, not having intended anything else, and she skimmed eagerly through the minutiae of domestic and county news, but paused over the last paragraph of the letter, reading it twice.

"Abe, Mary wants me to come home for a visit," she said slowly, as though thinking while she spoke, "she says Papa will pay the way. I haven't been back to Kentucky since we came away—nigh onto fifteen years."

"That would be a mighty nice trip for you," he offered sympathetically. "How is Miss Mary these days?" It might be idle curiosity, but he wanted very much to hear of Mary. He wanted to talk about her, to hear little, intimate stories of her. He wanted to clarify that blurred memory of her that he couldn't hardly recognize.

"Oh, she's still letting Papa wind her around his finger!" replied Betsey with exasperation. "She mustn't go here, and she oughtn't to do that, and no man in the whole state of Kentucky is good enough for his prize duckling! He never cared what the rest of us did—it was always Mary, Mary, Mary! I wonder my stepmother doesn't throw her right out of the house! Mary cares a great deal for Papa, but why shouldn't she? She hasn't anything else to care about!" She stopped her tirade abruptly, a calculating look stealing into her eyes. Mary and Abe hadn't taken to each other much when Mary was here. But now Abe was succeeding; and he was climbing up, no longer the good-natured indigent he had been then. Perhaps with a little out-and-out planning—

"Abe," she plunged, "you liked her when she was here, didn't you?"

"Of course. Who could help liking her?"

"Do you remember what you said after she left? You told me—"

"Seems to me I bragged that if she ever came back, I was going to marry her! It was a pretty big boast. But she didn't come back."

"Well, did you mean it?" she persisted. "Were you serious? If I went home to visit and brought her back, would you be—interested?"

Abe smiled. "She might have something to say about that herself."

"Oh Abe, don't be so exasperating! If I bring her back

with me, will you pay her some attention, and—and propose to her?"

He put on an air of great solemnity, not knowing whether to take her seriously or not. "I am honest, ma'am. My boasts are not given lightly."

Betsey laughed excitedly. "Then I'll go, Abe!" she promised. "I'll go, and bring you a bride!"

Walking back toward town, Abe reflected leisurely on Betsey's strange proposal. It might not be a bad idea. Not a bad idea at all . . . . .

Chapter Thirteen

$\mathcal{I}$T WAS AUTUMN 1836 BEFORE BETSEY FINALLY GOT OFF FOR her visit to Kentucky.

There had been the spring and summer farm work and the fall canning, and then she'd had to shop and sew in preparation for the journey. She wasn't going to have the family or the neighbors at home think that she and her husband weren't prosperous, and so she'd had to make a whole new wardrobe for herself. She couldn't do much about her personal looks any more, but her clothes were another matter.

During her crowded summer of planting, gardening, harvesting, and sewing, she had found little opportunity to talk with Abe. He was as busy as she, stumping up and down the county in his campaign for re-election.

He was in Springfield one day, in Salisbury another, and then she heard by the grapevine that he had made speeches in Mechanicsburg and all the towns about New Salem. There were barbecues and rallies at the farms nearby, for the farmers' votes were important. Abe was working in earnest, and leaving nothing to chance. From all reports he was doing it well, for every story of him that came back to Betsy confirmed her opinion formed years ago, that he would go far. He was becoming known for something besides his droll humor and his bad appearance. Older men, long experienced in politics, were listening to what he had to say about local and national affairs, and were finding his logic and his arguments sound.

He was still modest and straightforward, and honest. His new honors weren't going to his head, even though he was, as it were, drinking the first liquor of success on an empty stomach.

Betsy liked his announcement in the *Sangamo Journal* in June, in which he published his views:

".... I go for admitting all whites to the right of suffrage who pay taxes or bear arms (by no means excluding females).

"If elected, I shall consider the whole people of Sangamon my constituents, as well those that oppose me as those that support me....."

Only a few lines, but they came from a thinking man, a big man. Abe Lincoln was no two-bit politician. He was looking ahead to larger than local issues. He announced himself in favor of internal improvements on an empiric scale—canals and roads and railroads to open up the whole West, to build a mighty empire that could hold its own with the East and the South. But he couldn't keep his own dry humor out of his proclamation. He ended his letter to the editor of the paper with, "If alive on the first Monday in November, I shall vote for Hugh L. White for President." Well, that was like Abe Lincoln—so unassuming he wouldn't even claim to be alive in November!

Womanlike, Betsey considered Abe her own special discovery, and she became more determined than ever to make
a match between him and her sister: two lonely people, one
a beautiful, gently bred woman, and the other a man with a
purchase on genius; each possessed of qualities which could
complement the other's and make for their personal fulfilment.

"I don't want to arrange their lives," she argued honestly
with herself. "I only want to help them both to see what they
could find in each other."

She saw him once during the long summer, at a rally in
New Salem, in July.

The crowd was enormous, and Abe was in the center of it,
the heart of all the activity, the focus of all the attention and
enthusiasm. Surely, in all the history of the village, no man
had ever had so many friends!

Betsey had no opportunity to speak to him, but he caught
sight of her in the milling crowd, and waved, and his smile
was a recollection and a promise, and she was content.

On the long stagecoach journey—so different from her
trek fifteen years ago when she had come northwest with
Bennett—Betsey found herself remembering things she
hadn't thought of in years. The way her father sat at table
with his head turned half away from the food as though he
were listening for Indian attacks (a habit grown out of actual
danger when he himself was young and such an attack a
very real possibility). The tree that she and Mary had planted
on her sixteenth birthday—how tall would it be now? The

special teacakes concocted by some kind of witchcraft by a colored mammy now long dead. The smell of the locust trees in bloom.

And hers and Mary's long imaginings, after they had gone to bed at night, and were supposed to be asleep, about the kind of men they were going to marry. Betsey had thought then, in her early 'teens, that she'd like to marry a soldier, someone who went off to the wars and killed a lot of Indians, and came home periodically, unscathed, and covered with glory. But Mary wanted a prince, no less, or at the very lowest, a judge of the Circuit Court. The man who won Mary would have to beckon her from some high place, would have to offer her something bigger and better than her father had at home. Those were the secrets they whispered to each other, under cover of the dark that took away all embarrassment.

Betsey hadn't had to compromise too much with her girlish dream, she reflected as she watched the Indiana prairie jog by. A pioneer was a soldier of fortune, and right now Bennett was killing potato bugs rather than Indians, but he was moved by the same will to conquest as the man with the gun. And while there was less excitement in farming than in soldiering, there was a better satisfaction—a peace that came from producing living things instead of destroying them.

But Mary's dream? Betsey wondered how thin and emaciated her hope had become, and whether it was still alive at all, or had died for want of nourishment.

Mary was a strange person. During that brief visit three years ago, Betsey had hardly become acquainted with her.

Mary was everything that her father had brought her up to be. But, thought Betsey with some irritation and no impulse to pun, there was too much surface. Or rather, the surface was too impregnable. Betsey hadn't been able to see beyond it—it was like an impenetrable shell. She felt that she didn't really know Mary at all.

Well, this time she'd do better. This time she'd find some way to break the stranglehold Squire Owens had upon his daughter's thinking and affections. She didn't know just how she'd do it, but Abe Lincoln had always said that in wrestling the best maneuvers were the simplest—it was a matter of catching your opponent off-guard. But who was the real opponent here: Mary Owens or her father?

Then, as the horses' hooves pounded off the slow miles, Betsey thought, irrelevantly it seemed, about the magnolia tree that had shaded the window of hers and Mary's bedroom at home, and the heavy scent of the flowers wafting into the room on quiet spring nights.

Wistfully, she wondered if she were getting old. . . . .

Chapter Fourteen

"HE'S OLD," THOUGHT BETSEY, ALONE FOR A MOMENT IN Mary's room in the Big House after the excitement of greetings was over. "Papa's old, and for some reason, he's dependent on Mary. With a wife he's been married to for over twenty years, he still leans on Mary. It doesn't make sense, but there it is. Perhaps I shouldn't take her away from him."

Then, curious, she looked about Mary's retreat, that she was to share during her visit. And her ire rose again. For the room was as impersonal and virginal as though it had been lifted physically from that convent school her sister had attended, and fitted into the house. Prim and severe and ladylike, as stiff and uninviting as a cloister. Everything in its proper place, in spinsterish order. "I'd like to put a pair of men's carpet slippers under that bed and see if they'd liven the room up," Betsey thought, a little grimly. Then her heart twisted a little, for she spied, over on the window seat, Mary's last little-girl doll, propped against a baby pillow that must have belonged to one of the younger children. The doll was pantaletted and petticoated, and as correct and stiff as Mary herself. But the fact that Mary had kept the doll so carefully bore mute testimony to the fact of her thwarted maternal yearnings, and Betsey brushed aside all sympathy for her father in his old age. "He hasn't any right to keep her here, and ruin her life," she resolved. "I've just got to get her away!"

Ten-year-old Sarah, the "baby" of the Nathe Owens second family, whom Betsey had never seen until this visit, edged shyly into the room just then, and Betsey, in a rush of homesickness for her own children, took the solemn little girl into her arms, thanking God that her life was so much better than Mary's.

"Why, we're doing right well, Papa," Betsey explained later to her father, as she and Nathe, Miss Mary Ann and Mary sat about the early fire after dinner. The two little girls had gone to bed, and John had wandered off to visit with one of the neighbor boys. Betsey reflected silently that her own John, only a year younger than her half-brother, was a sight more self-reliant than this boy. Why, her John and Samuel were their father's right-hand men on the farm. It was all Bennett could do to keep up with them in the field. They were talking already about staking out some claims of their own. But Nathe Owens' John had prattled all through dinner about a new litter of coach dogs that some friend's bitch had dropped, and he wanted Papa to buy two for him. Betsey sighed over the pretty dresses that Margarite and Sarah were wearing—daintier, for every day, than her girls could wear on Sunday! Well, she reminded herself, there's more to living than dressing up fancy. My girls will know how to work and carry their end when they marry!

"We've got all the land under cultivation now," she went on, "though it was a hard pull until the boys got big enough to help. We're getting ahead, and the Sangamon is a wonderful country. People with any get-up just can't help doing well there! Why, we have one friend," she carefully avoided Mary's eyes, "who came to Illinois only six years ago, with no trade and no money, and only what learning he'd been able to get by himself, and he's been postmaster now for three years, and he learned surveying all on his own—though Cousin Mentor helped him—and he was appointed deputy surveyor and now he's just been re-elected to his second term in the state legislature!" She paused for breath. "His name's Lincoln, Papa. He came from somewhere around here. Do you recollect the family?"

Nathe Owens searched his memory. "The name sounds familiar. It seems to me there were some Lincolns—or Linkerns—over toward Knob Creek. They didn't amount to much, though. Fellow was so ignorant—must have been this chap's father—that he got his land titles all tangled up until even Richard Rudd, my friend over at Bardstown, couldn't straighten them out. They moved on. Weren't the kind to settle and stay."

He dismissed the whole family without another thought. Betsey was satisfied, for she had seen Mary perk up at the mention of Abe's name, and she knew that she had planted the first seeds of her intrigue. That was enough for tonight.

"How's my friend Zachariah Nance?" demanded her father. "And Thomas? Now there was a promising lad."

* * * *

The hills were too close. You couldn't see beyond half a mile for the round, low-brooding knobs. And the vegetation was too heavy, the trees crowding in upon her.

The land seemed overcultivated, like a garden geometrically planned. "I've grown away from it completely," Betsey told herself wonderingly. There was nothing left of her feeling for home except blood-ties of affection for her family. She had been wholly transplanted to Illinois.

The house was too old, and her father was too old. The darkies had grown stooped and slow in her father's service.

And yet, everything was the same, just as it had been when she lived here. Prayers before breakfast, with the master at the head of the table, and everyone in the house having to be there at the first word of the grace, as though they were still children. Betsey was used to getting up early in the morning, but she'd gotten out of the habit of obeisance.

She gossiped with the cook in the kitchen (a new one since she had lived at home), and helped Mary and Miss Mary Ann entertain the minister when he came to call. What girl friends were left in the neighborhood dropped around in the afternoon, rigged up in white gloves and bright-colored merinos and hats with plumes, as though they were going to the races. I wish they could see how we go calling on the spur of the moment to borrow a pound of sugar or a quilt pattern, in anything we happen to have on, and carrying the least ones along with us! But the mint juleps before dinner were nice. It was good to be waited on, to live leisurely for a while—just for a little while. Betsey had outgrown her capacity for gracious living, she thought.

She must get back to her own world, her own place. Her man and her children. She'd left the two least ones, who had come since Mary's visit to Illinois, with Jack Armstrong's wife. She'd hated to do it, but she couldn't have made the long trip with young ones, and now they were calling her back. It was good to see her people again, but this wasn't home. She must accomplish her purpose and go.

Strangely enough—for overanxious as she was to persuade Mary to return with her, she was almost sure she'd say the wrong thing—she hit on just the right remark to pique her sister's interest.

"Abe Lincoln was asking about you the last time I saw him," she said casually one day when she and Mary were in the garden cutting late flowers for the dinner table. "He asked me why I didn't bring you back with me. Did I ever tell you that right after you left he vowed that if you ever came again he'd marry you?"

Mary stopped her flower cutting and stood very still for a moment. "Did he really say that?"

"Of course he did! I wouldn't story you! He said it the week after you left. He came out to see you, and you weren't there. He said, 'If that young woman ever returns from Kentucky I'm going to catch, tie, and marry her!'"

Something of Mary's fine spirit came back, and she tossed her head defiantly. "Perhaps I'm not so easily caught as that, Betsey! Perhaps that over-confident young man needs showing!"

Betsey breathed a very silent sigh of relief. Mary would go back with her to Illinois.

Chapter Fifteen

*F*OLKS WHO WERE THERE SAID, YEARS LATER, THAT THEY had never in their lives seen anything as striking as Mary Owens when she got off the stagecoach at New Salem with her sister.

This was the presidential election day, Van Buren against White, the Whig for whom Abe Lincoln had promised in writing to vote for "if he lived," and the village was packed with people from the whole country round. If she had planned a triumphal entry into New Salem, Mary couldn't have done better.

Those who knew her from her first visit, and those who didn't, stared open-mouthed, and stopped talking politics. She wasn't exactly beautiful, for she was above ordinary height, inclined to be matronly beyond her years; but her blue eyes were lovely, and she wore the finest trimmings the little town had ever witnessed, and carried herself like royalty.

Squire Owens' wealth had never been a secret in New Salem, though Betsey didn't brag about it, and the Abells had apparently always lived on their own. While they were substantial, they didn't put on any great show of prosperity.

Mary Owens was different. Every garment she wore, every movement she made, offered proof incontrovertible of her gentle background, of the luxury in which she had been reared.

The married men about town bemoaned their fetters when they saw her, and those who were happily single began to think about matrimony.

But before any of the local swains could change their shirts to go courting her, Abe Lincoln was there, and he acted right serious. . . . .

He had promised Betsey, and he didn't aim to lose any time. Still, preparing for his first meeting with Mary, Abe was troubled. Had he been a little hasty in his bargain, promising to take a bride almost "sight unseen"? For almost all he knew of Mary was what Betsey had told him. He hadn't gotten acquainted with her during her short visit three years ago. He'd been interested in her, but hardly seriously, because at that time he was in no position to be serious about any woman.

Well, he'd given his word, and he must keep it. He was thankful, as he walked out to the Abell farm, that his clothes weren't as shabby and ill-fitting as those he'd worn the last time she saw him, and he knew, too, that he was quite a different person from the confused, groping backwoodsman he'd been then. He was a member of the Legislature now, tried and found worth returning to represent his people. Older and wiser men listened to him now, and sometimes even agreed with him. He had the self-assurance of a small but growing success, and a brightly burning belief in his future. Now, he had something to offer Mary.

But—women. Would any man ever completely understand them? Would Mary be pleased with what he had been making of himself, or would she compare him, to his disadvantage, with the country gentlemen at home who knew which horse to bet on and how to hold a whiskey glass? Well, he reflected, fancy gentlemen there might be in Green County, but she hadn't married one yet!

However, searching his memory of her, he decided that she would be kind, and interested, and glad of his moderate success, whether she wanted to marry him or not.

As he neared the farm, he forgot his self-consciousness in his eagerness to see her again. She was the fairy princess from the great castle, and he was going to court and marry her. . . . .

She was older, he thought, and heavier, but she still possessed the charm that had fascinated him before, that self-assurance that was consciousness of worth, of value in herself and everything that had made her what she was. It was the quality of bluegrass and clover bloom and leisure, with an indefinable something that must be just woman-ness.

She greeted Abe cordially, as though she were genuinely glad of his coming.

"Mr. Lincoln! How nice to see you again!" She gave him her hand, and the touch of it was like satin.

He stammered something, and knew that he was being clumsy again, but she went on speaking as though she hadn't noticed.

"You are to be highly congratulated for your re-election to the Legislature. Your constituents must have been pleased with your record." Somehow, her language didn't seem pedantic, for she spoke so easily, so softly.

"I'm mighty pleased with my re-election, Miss Mary," he replied gravely, "a re-election is almost more important than a first election, for as you say, it means the people are satisfied. I tried to represent them honestly."

She smiled, but the conversation lagged a little. Abe wondered where Betsey was. Certainly, she shouldn't have deserted him during his first call. She'd promised to help him with this affair! "How did you leave your father and the family?" he asked at last, remembering her devotion to the Squire.

She plunged eagerly into a recital of trivia from the plantation—things he could neither understand nor find interest in, and his doubts returned. Wasn't she being overcordial? Just a little too eager to impress him? Could Betsey have told her of their "understanding"?

For the first time, he began to realize the seriousness of that bargain. A promise, lightly given, that could affect all the rest of his life. Nevertheless, a promise was a promise. Strange as the pledge was, he'd keep it, come hell, tornado, or the Democrats. But he wished Betsey would come in and take charge. . . . .

Abe Lincoln danced attendance on Betsey Abell's guest so assiduously that the whole town was amazed, amused, and highly interested.

They'd never seen him chase a woman before, and speculation ran wild as to the seriousness of his intentions and his chances of success.

From all anybody knew, he'd never taken a marrying interest in any woman. Of course, some said he'd carried on bad when Jim Rutledge's girl died, but Abe was so soft-hearted he mourned when any little thing died—a bird, or a kitten, or a girl. And who in the village didn't feel down-right terrible when little Ann, with her auburn curls and her gentle ways, had wasted away—over a lover who never came back? Moreover, Abe Lincoln wasn't one to take squatter's rights on another man's property, even if the owner wasn't looking after his claim. Abe had never courted the innkeeper's daughter, but he sure as hell was courting Miss Owens.

He was out there at the Abell farm early and late, day after day, until folks gave up looking for him anywhere else. If anybody sought him to mail a letter or draw a deed, some wit at the Tavern or at Sam Hill's was sure to say, "Walk out north of town about a mile'n a half to Bennett Abell's. You'll likely find him there."

Some pledged bets for, and some against, the local Lothario. "She's a fine lady, and mighty proud. She wouldn't be willing to settle in this wild country." "She's use' to high life in Kaintucky. Abe caint step lively enough for her."

The majority of the townsfolk, however, was pulling for Abe to win. He was idolized by men, women, and children, and he was good enough for a king's daughter, if that was what he wanted. And the woman who couldn't see his worth just wasn't good enough for him. That was the way the people of New Salem looked at Abe Lincoln.

Chapter Sixteen

*A*BE WAS BITTERLY DISAPPOINTED OVER THE OUTCOME OF the election which gave the presidency to Martin Van Buren.

He discussed it with Mary at length, knowing that she could hardly have grown up in Kentucky without becoming both informed on and interested in politics. Moreover, he had found her an able conversationalist, her mind trained far beyond that of the average woman. He could talk to her about the things that interested a man.

"White's candidacy, along with Harrison's and Judge McLean's and Daniel Webster's, were all part of a plot," he explained to her, "to break up the vote so much that the election would have to be thrown into the House of Representatives. I reckon your father told you all about it. He must have known. Everybody knew. But it didn't work. Jackson had built up too good a patronage system. I suppose you know I voted for White," he added. "I didn't make any bones about it, before my own election."

"Papa did too," she replied, "though I saw by the Lo'ville paper that Kentucky went for Harrison. That's rather surprising, for Kentuckians don't usually trust anyone who lives no'th of the Ohio River, you know."

"No, I didn't know. I was just a shaver when I left Kentucky."

Mary explained to him: "It's much more natural that a Kentuckian should vote for a Tennessee man, as Papa did, than for one from Ohio—or the East. Kentucky and Tennessee were settled by Virginians like Papa, or folks from the Carolinas. Papa says that Ohio and Indiana are just outgrowths of New England Puritanism and industrialism. I hear there's talk of a resolution in the Senate to investigate the voting."

"It won't do any good," replied Abe gloomily, "even if the vote was close. Jackson's handed out his plums so smart that he's built up a dynasty he thinks will last forever. He chose Van Buren—the people didn't. He wants to run the country as long as he lives—and from his grave after that. And it's a funny thing, but the people seem to want him to do it. They're afeared of 'Biddle's Bank.' Seems like they don't even want stable currency. They want Ohio money in Ohio and Illinois money in Illinois—and buckskin pelts all points west of the Mississippi. They think the Bank is some kind of 'control' that will rob them of their right to run after other men's wives."

"There was a great deal of talk at home about the Bank," Mary remarked thoughtfully, "but I didn't follow much of it. Women will never understand national finance—not even if they get the franchise some day. Because they think in small, intimate terms: the cost of a spool of thread, or a side of pork, or a yard of calico."

What a strange creature she was! Lincoln thought admiringly. One minute she was all intellect, discussing politics like a man, and the next, she was utterly and deliciously feminine, talking of the little things that make up a woman's life! He told himself he was confoundedly well pleased with the bargain he'd struck with Betsey. He couldn't have picked a better candidate for companionship if he'd done the choosing himself.

Mary was wonderfully easy to talk to. Abe found himself telling her about his first home on Little Nolin, and the Indiana years, and his mother.

"I don't recollect much about my mother," he sighed, "except she always seemed tired. Folks said I took after her in looks. Sarah Bush, my father's second wife, took my side against Pap when he thought I was wastin' my time readin' books. Sarah was mighty good to us."

Mary liked his kind reference to his stepmother. That experience, at least, was one that she shared with him.

"Us?" she inquired.

"My sister Sarah," he explained. "She was a few years older'n me. She died, back in Indianny."

A closed look came into his face, and Mary thought it was from sorrow, and did not press him for details.

Abe couldn't tell her more, for he was remembering how Sarah had died of childbed fever, and that thought brought back to him a horror and fear of marriage itself, and the responsibility of a man for the things that marriage could do to a woman. He knew, reasonably, that it was poverty and lack of medical care that had killed his sister, but the revulsion remained with him, for Sarah might have survived the hardship if childbirth hadn't been added to her difficulties.

He changed the subject abruptly, and told Mary about little Katy Robey. "I reckon I thought I was in love with her. I was about fourteen. But she was a nice girl. She's probably married now, with a half a dozen young'uns."

He told her also of an incident which would have been screamingly funny, if it weren't so touching.

Abe had been riding over the prairie, he said, rather "fixed up," when he came upon a hog mired down in the mud. There wasn't a human being in sight, just him and that hog, out in the wilderness. Not thinking much about the animal, he had ridden on, but when he got well past something had made him look back at her.

"And would you believe it, Miss Mary," he recounted with a wry smile, "that hawg was lookin' at me with her heart in her eyes, just as if she was thinkin', 'There goes my last hope.' So I'll be daggoned if I didn't go back, and get off my horse and down into the mud, and pull her out. I couldn't finish my errand, because I was splattered from one end to the other. But I felt better than if I'd left her there to die."

That story stirred something close to tears in her heart, this compassion of a man who had never known comfort himself, for a dumb animal mired down in the mud. . . . .

The weather was unusually mild that autumn, and Abe and Mary went for long walks in the flaming woods. There was little else they could do if they wanted to be alone.

They wandered aimlessly, talking or silent, as the mood

urged, sometimes stopping to watch the wild birds and animals getting ready for winter, preparing for the long rest before mating again in the spring.

It was such a walk and such a day that impelled Abe to plunge into his proposal.

He'd just come back from Springfield, where a group of Sangamon County citizens had gathered to talk over the need for internal improvements within the county. Abe had gone because he wanted to know just what the people wanted, before he should return to Vandalia. He'd come back full of enthusiasm and that feeling of power and confidence that contact with politics and politicians always gave him. Now was the time to propose to Mary, while he was feeling good, and sure of himself.

When they came upon a fallen log in the woods, Abe asked Mary to stop and sit a spell.

"There's something I've been aiming to ask you about, Miss Mary," he stumbled, "and I don't know any pretty words or nice phrases, so I reckon I'll just have to spit it out. I haven't got much to offer any woman yet, but I may have some day. I think I'll have. In the meantime, my wife might have to live in a house nowhere near as good as Betsey's, and work like no white woman ought to work, and have faith in me even when she couldn't see over the next hill. Do you think you could stand that?"

Mary sat very still, looking down at her hands. So this was it! This was it, Abe Lincoln's proposal. She had known it was coming. She had known, and wondered. Wondered what her answer would be.

She knew quite well what he meant by the hardships that

might attend marriage to him, at least for a few years. For Betsey had told her how meager his earnings were, in spite of his growing reputation. She understood, too, that political success was a precarious thing, and that a politician might lose, overnight, what it had taken him years to gain. She believed, on the other hand, that worldly success would come to him more quickly if he had the right kind of woman to help him. A woman who knew social procedure, a woman who could smooth off—or compensate for—his own rough corners. But would marriage to Abe Lincoln bring her, Mary Owens, any personal fulfilment? That would depend on Abe, himself.

She looked up into his face at last, and her wide eyes were very blue.

"I could stand any kind of hardship, Abe, if I loved and were loved. But if my suitor were at all doubtful of his feelings for me, I would rather spend my life as a spinster in my father's house."

Surely, if he loved her, he would say so now! And if he said he loved her, she could forget all his faults, forget the luxury of her home, and follow him, her man, as Betsey had followed Bennett, over half a world, through hardships that were not hard at all because they were together.

She looked for a long time into his grey eyes, and when he said nothing, she turned her face away, staring out into the darkening woods.

The curve of her neck was so soft. Her curls were so pretty! When she had looked at him just now, her eyes so wide, her red lips half parted, had she expected him to kiss her? God knew, he wanted to. But could a man kiss a nice girl before she gave him her answer? Abe didn't know. No one had ever told him.

I'll do it anyhow, he thought. I'll take her in my arms and kiss her, and sweep her off her feet. She'll have to love me then!

He stretched out a hand toward her, but the very thought of touching her as a lover confused him so, set his blood to pounding so violently, that he was afraid. He knew quite well what desire could do to him. There was no telling what those hands of his might do—those calloused, work-worn hands. Were they fit to caress any woman? Oh God, he wished he knew what she wanted, what she really expected of him!

He drew back, trembling, and only his strangled breath could tell his emotion.

"Mary—"

"Yes, Abe?" Her voice was very quiet, but she wouldn't look at him. Why couldn't she help him a little?

"Mary," he forced steadiness into his voice, "if you risk your future and your happiness with me, I'll do everything in my power to keep you from regretting it. You know that, don't you?"

"Yes, I know it." Indeed, she did know. The sincerity of his intentions could never be doubted. However, Mary Owens, lonely, no longer young, wanted love more than she wanted predictions of conduct. She wanted love as she wanted air to breathe. And unless he loved her enough to say so, what could marriage with him mean?

"Abe," she told him at last, "I can't give you an answer

now. I appreciate your offer deeply, but I'll have to think about it. You'll allow me a little time, won't you?"

She was very gentle, very sweet, wholly reasonable. But with her pleading for time, all his confusion returned, and his terrible self-doubt.

She was quite right, no woman should plunge into a life partnership without due deliberation. But the moment was gone. He was bewildered, embarrassed.

"All right, Mary," he said quietly, "take all the time you want. But my word is good. You'll find that out. Now, it's time we were getting home."

He helped her up from the log, and they walked back to the Abell farm as though they'd been talking all afternoon about taxes.

Chapter Seventeen

THE GROUP ABOUT SAM HILL'S STORE HAD RUN OUT OF TALK. Peter Cartwright, sprawled as usual on the steps, had finished a long and derogatory tirade against drinking in general and Sam Hill in particular, and since most of the others owed Sam money and didn't have much against him anyhow, the talk bogged down to speculation about the weather.

Dr. Allen had just scurried up the street with his black bag, throwing an angry glance back over his shoulder that seemed to corroborate all of Peter's remarks, and made the whole bunch feel as though they'd had guilt forced upon them through no act of their own.

The election was over, the fall work done, and there was no excitement, nothing to look forward to but the long, hard prairie winter.

"Seems like we should'a had a revival meetin' this fall," mused Jack Kelso, for once lured back to the world of men, mostly because it was too cold to go fishing.

"Lot you'd do at a revival meeting besides get drunk," accused Peter. "You can do that without no revival meeting."

"I know, but it's good to have a reason. Revivals, and elections, and birthin's, and funerals. My God, do you see what I see?"

They all followed his glance across the street. Along the road that led in from Rutledge's Tavern loped Abe Lincoln, looking in the distance quite as usual—more like a crane than a man—but as he came nearer, they saw the reason for Jack's amazement.

"Two galluses he's wearin'." The remark was uttered in awe, in perfect bewilderment. "Both pant legs are hangin' alike."

"And a stovepipe hat like a drunken Senator!"

Abe was close enough now so that they could see the results of blacking and elbow grease on his boots.

"That I should live to see the day!" exclaimed Jack, still wondering if the sight wasn't an alcoholic apparition of his own. It couldn't be Abe, his old fishing pal, his good companion who had found more delight with him in the sonnets of Shakespeare than in concerns of raiment or even food. "It's a travesty!" reverting to the book words that he used in his thoughts, but seldom in his speech.

"Travesty, nothin'! It's a downright crime! And it's all the doin' of that fancy sister-in-law of Bennett Abell's!"

Sam Hill, having been married to Parthena Nance, the Owens girls' best friend, felt that he was almost one of Abell's family, and started to defend Abe's courtship, but just then Lincoln came alongside the store, and the conversation stopped.

Abe didn't stop. He tilted the tall hat at a more rakish angle, and asked, "Anything in the post office I should take care of, Sam?" Learning that there wasn't, he pranced on up the street.

"On the way to Bennett's again, and he ain't dressed for farmin'!" observed Peter disconsolately.

"I kind of hate to see him get roped and tied," reflected Jack, convinced now that Abe was real and not a product of *delirium tremens*. "I've got nothin' against matrimony,"— he shouldn't have, thought Sam sourly, with the wife he's got!—"but somehow, if Abe was to marry, it would seem like hitchin' an eagle to a hand-plow. No matter who the woman was."

There was no answer to that, for there was no argument possible. It was certain, just as certain as the fact that, for the time being at least, they had lost their comrade—to a woman. Their pride was hurt. And what was more, they missed him.

Abe was in high spirits today. Maybe it was the broadcloth shirt he was wearing. Maybe it was the thin, winey November air. Maybe it was the prospect of return to Vandalia. It might have been Mary. . . . .

He had rationalized his first hurt at her hesitancy (it had hurt his pride more than anything else), and had even convinced himself that he could understand her unwillingness to plunge into marriage with a man who had little to offer her but dreams. For if marriage was a desperate affair for a man, it must be equally cataclysmic for a woman. She was a gentle person, and she had a right to be cautious. However, humble though he felt in most things, he hadn't the slightest doubt of her final answer. Given plenty of time, plenty of room, there was only one decision she could make, for Abe believed in his dream, and he believed that Mary understood that dream and gave it credence, too.

Perhaps today, perhaps tomorrow, sometime soon, she would say yes, she would come into his arms today. . . . .

Perhaps today. . . . .

He found Betsey alone when he reached the farm. Mary, she said, had gone calling by her own self, this time to see Nancy Green, Bowling's wife, who, being "home folks," wasn't to be neglected. Betsey had stayed behind, preoccupied with morning sickness again.

"Why don't you go over and fetch her back?" suggested Betsey shamelessly. "You're certainly not fixed up to go tramping around the farm with Bennett."

"Well, I really wasn't aimin' to clean the cow barn," he admitted, displaying his shining boots with pride. "You sure Miss Mary won't be put out if I tag her over there?"

"You'll never convince her of your interest if you sit around waiting for her!" Betsey retorted with spirit. Men were such blockheads! She wondered if she ought to write a speech for him to recite to Mary. He was downright brilliant when he talked politics, but she had a suspicion that if he had proposed to Mary at all, he'd said all the wrong things, and left the right words unsaid. She was burning with curiosity to know how the courtship was really coming, and yet it was a pretty personal thing. She didn't want to upset a delicate balance by prying. Just the same, it might be a long time before she had a chance to talk to him alone again. She'd have to chance it. After all, they were in this business together.

Nevertheless, she stammered when she asked him, "Abe,— how is it going? Have you—"

Abe stammered too. "She wants time, Betsey. She said she wanted to be sure. I want her to be, too." Then, embarrassed at having given that much confidence, even to Betsey, who was his co-conspirator, he edged toward the door. "I reckon I better get along toward Bowling's, before some dandy beats me there."

And he was out of the yard, striding down the road, for all the world as though he'd just inherited a house and lot.

Time, indeed! thought Betsey angrily after he had gone. Mary had to have time! Well, Mary didn't have any time to spend, making up her mind! She was twenty-eight years old, and—with a flash of disloyalty for which she was instantly sorry—twenty-five pounds over-weight, and if there were any better or even other suitors hanging around her doorstep, Betsey had neither seen nor heard anything about them! Here, Mary had a chance for the lifelong devotion of a man with so much ambition and ability that he might even be governor some day, and she had to have time to think about it! Mary was simply insane, or else so conceited that she thought getting a husband, at her age, was simply a matter of making up her own mind.

Something would simply have to be done to hurry the courtship along. But Betsey couldn't think, at the moment, what it could be. For talking to Mary would do no good at all. Betsey would only be reminded, if she tried to plead

Abe's case for him, that Mary was capable of doing her own thinking and of making her own decisions. No, there was nothing Betsey could do to urge on the climax. She would just have to let it run its course, and hope for the right outcome.

Moreover, at this particular moment, the baby was crying, the bread dough overrunning the pan, and Betsey's world was reeling with the familiar nausea which, somehow, didn't lessen with repetition.

As he had hoped, Mary welcomed Abe warmly when he arrived at Bowling Green's. One might almost hazard a guess that she had expected him. But that didn't dampen his spirits. Abe was riding a high wave of confidence these days, and nothing could break the wave.

"You came just in time to walk back with me to the farm," she greeted him brightly. "And I'm so glad, because I don't like tramping across the fields alone." Then, as if she felt she had been too eager, she added to Bowling's wife, "Nancy, why don't you come with us? Betsey wasn't feeling well enough to come over, and I'm sure she'd be glad to see you!"

Nancy Green hesitated. There was work to do, she didn't want to leave her baby alone, and she rightly guessed that Abe wanted his lady to himself. But Abe good-naturedly added his pleas to Mary's insistence, and Nancy let herself be persuaded. "I'll just have to take the baby, though," she told them. "He's too fussy to leave here."

They all started out over the stubbled field, Abe trying hard to match his long stride to the women's gait, relating all the town news as he went.

"I've been working on a petition to the county commissioners asking for a county road from Middletown to the county line," he told them.

That didn't mean much to Mary except that the townspeople of New Salem thought enough of Abe's ability to ask him to draw the petition, but Nancy was immediately interested. "Where will the road go? Will it run anywhere near here? Do you think we'll get it?"

Abe tried to answer one question at a time. "Well, it's thought the best place to start it would be near Musick's bridge, and then to Meadow's Mill at Sugar Grove, and then on to the county line. It would be a mighty fine thing. But whether we get it or not is another matter. This isn't the only section that wants and needs roads."

"I believe we need 'em worse than anybody," sighed Nancy.

"That's what every constituency thinks," replied Abe drily.

They had come by now to a brook running lazily through the pasture, which had to be crossed on stepping stones. The water was low, and there was no danger in crossing, but the stones were irregularly placed, some close together and some far apart, and they were difficult to negotiate. Mary lagged behind Abe and Nancy, thinking that of course he would help Nancy because of the baby she was carrying. But Abe, his thoughts anywhere but on the women, leaped nimbly across without even looking back to see whether the girls were coming.

Mary was incensed. "Nancy, give me the baby!" she demanded. "You've carried him long enough!"

"I'm used to carrying him," Nancy refused. She sensed Mary was trying to call Abe to his manners, and she didn't want him embarrassed. Moreover, she was sympathetic to this match, and if it should develop as she hoped, Mary would soon enough have the burdens of child care. Anyhow, what did a small discourtesy like that matter!

When they came to a hill about three-quarters of a mile farther on, the heavy baby became increasingly burdensome. Nancy wished she'd left him at home, or that she'd stayed at home herself. During the ascent, Abe suddenly became solicitous of Mary. Nancy didn't mind Abe's thoughtlessness, but halfway up the hill, she had to stop to rest, and to shift the baby from one arm to the other. Abe waited politely for Nancy to get her breath, but he kept on with his clumsy attempts to help Mary.

It was more than Mary could stand. She waited until they reached the top of the hill—hoping all the way up that Abe would come to his senses and give Nancy a lift—and then she burst out. After all, knowing enough to help a woman with a heavy child wasn't a matter of drawing-room experience, it was just common sense!

"Abe," she told him, "didn't it even occur to you to carry that baby up the hill for Nancy?"

"Why—well, I guess it didn't," he floundered. "I reckon I was thinking of something else."

"You must have been!" stormed Mary. "And what could be so important to think of that could make you so inconsiderate?"

Her anger was so new to him, so startling, that Abe was bewildered and confused. For one thing, he had been think-

ing of Mary. Anyhow, this wasn't Green County, Kentucky.
Nancy had gone on ahead, so he could speak out.

"Mary, Nancy is a pioneer woman, who doesn't expect
her husband's friends to tote her children for her. She probably never gave it a thought. This isn't the old plantation
here in Illinois. It's pioneer country, where a man is taken
for his worth and not for his manners! And I never pretended to you to be a polished gentleman!" The last, with a
little bitterness that he could not conceal.

Mary, amazed that he should even try to defend his action,
tried to explain. "There are different kinds of manners,
Abe," she said. "Some are entirely a matter of social procedure, like how to seat guests at a dinner for the governor.
But good sense and common consideration for others, particularly for women, are just a matter of elementary decency.
I don't believe that kind of thoughtfulness should be limited
to locality!"

Abe, lashed by her scorn, apologized, and told her humbly
that he was just absent-minded, he hadn't thought, and that
he'd try to remember.

The day was spoiled. The keen edge of his enjoyment,
even his self-confidence, was blunted, and though he stopped
for a while at the Abell place, he and Mary parted with irritation still between them, neither one very happy.

Chapter Eighteen

IT WAS A VERY INSIGNIFICANT INCIDENT, LINCOLN TOLD HIM-self, but he could not dismiss it from his memory. Mary's scorn rankled and hurt, like a thorn so deeply embedded in his flesh that it could not be removed.

It was all very well to argue that she was unfair in expect-ing him to know the niceties of behavior to which she had been brought up, that he had never had an opportunity to learn the ways of gentlemen. The truth still remained that Mary had been right, and that the procedure in question had been a matter of common consideration and not of training. Any man, even a "Linkern," should have known that.

On the other hand, Mary was not engaged to him, she had refused to give him a definite answer, and so what right had she to criticize, what claim had she upon him that allowed her to sit in judgment on his acts?

Try as he would to quiet his conscience, however, he still felt his defection, and his feelings pendulummed between longing to see her again—to try to explain, to ask her for-giveness—and embarrassment that became angry resentment.

He kept up his mental debate for a couple of days, and

then circumstance stepped in with an opportunity for him to go to Havana on a surveying job.

He welcomed the definiteness of the work and the chance to get away from his problem for a while. A spell out in the open might clear his head and straighten out his thoughts.

And a little time without his attention might be good for his high-handed lady friend. . . . .

When Betsey insisted and insisted, Mary finally told her why Abe had gone off surveying without even calling to say goodbye. The girls didn't even know of his departure until Bennett came back from a trip to the village and mentioned having heard it.

"It was humiliating," Mary told her sister after she had recounted the incident. "I don't know how anyone, even a— a backwoodsman—could be so ignorant! And when I took him to task about it, he made it worse! He said that pioneer women didn't expect courtesy, and that Nancy was used to toting her babies! What kind of a husband could he possibly make?"

Betsey was in the unfortunate position of being able to see both sides of the problem. And she knew men a great deal better than her sister.

"Of course you're right, Mary," she soothed, "but you shouldn't have snapped at him. It hurt his pride. You can't drive any man, Mary. But you can lead most of them. And believe me—I know Abe—and he's very conscious of his deficiencies and anxious to make up for them."

"Then why did he say that in pioneer country, common

decency is neither expected nor welcomed?" demanded Mary.

"Well, he's right when he says it isn't expected," returned Betsey. "There isn't time to be mannerly when you're trying to squeeze a living out of a stump field. But did you ever know a man who understood women? Even Papa?"

Mary remembered the affectionate but exacting obeisance that Nathe Owens demanded of his women, and secretly reckoned Betsey was right. Nathe Owens gave a great deal in return for that obeisance, but her honesty told her that he had a great deal to give. It makes a man feel like God to be generous, particularly when he has so much largess that he can give without inconvenience to himself.

Her mental debating made her feel no better. She still felt that her attitude, if not her procedure, was right—so right that it was wrong! She was confused, and she didn't like feeling wrong when she knew she was right. Betsey had made her feel that the social blunder was hers in not understanding Abe better. She knew, too, that she had hurt him, deliberately, and that Abe Lincoln, gentleman or not as she had been taught to construe the term, would never knowingly hurt any living thing. . . . .

It was young Sam Abell who saw Abe first, when the surveyor finally returned to the village from his trip.

The first place Abe went was to Sam Hill's, to look after the mail that had accumulated in his absence, and there was the Abell boy buying sugar and coffee for his mother, and looking longingly at the whiskey mugs of the older men. When would he be old enough to take a friendly drink, like the grownups did? speculated young Sam. Ma had told him that when she was years younger than he, she had had egg-nogs at home on Christmas day, but she didn't seem to think that was whiskey. Well, she couldn't keep him from a chew of tobacco now and then, and he could spit like a man. He could hit Sam Hill's goboon at ten feet.

He'd just made a ringer, and was edging closer to the group of men about the barrel to listen to their big talk, when Abe strolled in, muddy, needing a shave, needing sleep. Sam forgot all about trying to act grown up, and rushed over to greet his friend.

"Abe, you were gone a long time! What were you doin'?"

"Markin' off a piece of land over Havana way," replied Abe, talking to the boy as though he were his own height and age. "It took a mite longer'n I reckoned on."

"Abe, take me with you next time! Let me go along, will you? I could—well, I could carry things for you! Take me with you!" Sam sensed adventure in Abe's surveying trips which was no less attractive because it was entirely imagined. "I could learn to be a surveyor, too! George Washin'ton wasn't much older'n me when he learned!"

"I guess he wasn't," agreed Abe soberly, knowing better than to laugh at a boy in his teens, and then, judging he'd waited long enough so that he wouldn't seem over-eager, "How's your folks?"

"Oh, they're all right. Ma's ailin' again. Same old thing ever' day on the farm—milk the cows, take 'em out to pasture, clean the barn, haul water, haul wood, mend fences. I wisht I was a surveyor an' a represen'ative maybe goin' to be governor!"

"How's Miss Mary?" persisted Abe, ignoring the boy's effusion.

"Oh, she's busy gaddin' around the country," replied Sam. "Or talkin' to Ma about how things used to be when they were both home in Kaintuck' an' had darkies to wait on 'em hand an' foot. I never saw a darky. What're they like?"

"Very like you and me," replied Abe, "except that their skins are dark. And sometimes I think they're happier. They have a great capacity for happiness, Sam. They have to have, for they live only in the present. They have nothing to look forward to."

Sam wasn't quite up to sociological considerations. He was still thinking about surveying. "Would it take me long to learn? To be a surveyor? Would it?"

Abe smiled down at the boy from his great height. "It took me a long time, but perhaps you'd learn faster. Are you going home now?"

"Well, pretty soon, if Sam ever gets his face out of the whiskey bar'l long enough to wrap me up some sugar an' coffee."

"Then tell your aunt that I'll be out to see her as soon as I get fixed up, will you?"

Abe went then to look over the mail, and young Sam gazed after him sorrowfully. Women! Thinkin' about women! Abe Lincoln, the greatest man in the world prit-near, runnin' hisse'f in circles tryin' to please a woman, even if she was Sam's own kin! Well, Sam would never rig himse'f up like a senator an' go traipsin' all over the county after a female! There was men's work to do in the world, like

Indian shooting and surveying and getting to be represen'a-tive and maybe governor!

Sam spat at the goboon again, missed, and strolled disconsolately outside. Everything was wrong since Aunt Mary came this time. The boys had to sleep three-four in a bed, and they had to wet their hair down for dinner till it looked like they'd put bear's grease on it, and they had to wait on her like she was the Queen of England. And now Abe Lincoln was making a fool of himself over her! "I'd like to find me a island and live there, where there ain't any women a-tall," he brooded. Then he remembered that Ma was baking today, and wondered how soon his groceries would be ready so that he could start back. . . . . .

Inside the store, Abe tackled the mail with a light heart. Everything was going to be all right, after all. He'd been wrong that day coming home from the Bowling Green's, and he'd tell Mary so, and everything would be fine!

Chapter Nineteen

$\mathcal{W}$ELL, HE SAID HE'S COMIN', AN' I TOLD YOU, AND THAT'S all I care," Sam told his aunt. He grabbed another doughnut from the big wooden bowl on the table, and made for the barn, where life was predictable.

Betsey didn't like the thin, tight line around Mary's mouth, so she poured herself a cup of coffee and sat down at the table to gather her forces.

"You don't have to go to Cousin Mentor's today, Mary," she opened up.

"I'm afraid I do," Mary replied. "They're expecting me, and we've made other plans for the rest of the week. I'm going."

"Mary!" protested Betsey, knowing it would do no good, for when Mary got into one of these hard-to-handle moods, there was no persuading her, "if you go away after he's sent you word he's coming, it will be just the last straw! Abe Lincoln isn't a man you can play cat and mouse with!"

Mary's mouth only got stubborner. "He left without sending any word," she reminded her sister, "and he stayed away until he got right good and ready to come back. But he thinks that all he has to do is send out a command, and I'll upset all my plans and wait for him! Who does he think he is—the president?"

"Oh Mary!" Betsey floundered helplessly. "It doesn't matter what he thinks as long as he likes you, does it?"

"It matters to me what I think. I've made my plans to go to the Grahams today, and I'm going. Your Mr. Lincoln evidently doesn't understand the importance of keeping one's social engagements. There's a very great deal that he doesn't understand. And," it was a last-minute inspiration—"if he's so anxious to see me, he can come along over. The Grahams are his friends, too."

That ought to be a real test, she gloated inwardly. If he really wanted to heal their quarrel, let him put himself out a little, instead of expecting her to dance to whatever tune he chose to play! "When he comes, Betsey, tell him where I am. Tell him that the Grahams are expecting me, that I have to keep my word, but that if he likes, he may come and fetch me home."

Betsey didn't like it at all, but there was nothing she could do. There was no holding Mary, no convincing her that Abe wasn't giving her "commands" but was taking it for granted that she'd be glad enough to see him to push other plans aside for him after he'd been away for so many days. You couldn't tell Mary anything. She would do as she pleased, in spite of hell and high water.

"But I can't tell him she deliberately went away when she knew he was coming," Betsey told herself when Mary had gone. "He just wouldn't understand. If this thing is ever to be straightened out, somebody has got to use some sense. And it's perfectly clear that neither Abe nor Mary will!"

She was getting tired of trying to run a love affair that was like a run-away colt and wouldn't take to harness. Well, she'd try once more to patch it up and give them another chance.

Abe came in with little Oliver dangling from one hand, and the boy was talking two-forty.

"I heard Sam tell her you were coming, but she went off anyhow," Oliver was saying. "She acted like she was kinda mad. But you can visit with us. You can tell me about Black Hawk an' the 'Talisman'—" Abe's adventures ran all together in the little boy's mind, as though they'd happened simultaneously. And he was delighted at the prospect of having Abe "visit with us," and pay some attention to him instead of talking to Aunt Mary all the time.

But Abe brushed him aside, and confronted Betsey. "She knew I was coming," he accused her, as though it were Betsey's fault. "Oliver heard Sam tell her so."

"She'd told the Grahams she was coming," Betsey blundered. "They were expecting her, and she felt she had to keep her word. Why don't you go on over and bring her back?"

"No." He had been gone over two weeks, and he'd asked her to wait here for his call today. She'd seen the Grahams constantly, ever since her arrival. They weren't so important, even if they were kin! The way folks ran back and forth visiting each other here, it wasn't like a "social engagement" that demanded keeping. Even Mary's exaggerated social sense didn't require that. No, she had gone because she wanted to go, because she was still angry at him, and wanted to hurt him.

"I'll go along back to town," he told Betsey against her urging that he wait for Mary, or at least visit with the family for a while. "I don't feel much for visiting."

On the long walk back to the village, even the early moon, peeking around the bluff, seemed to be laughing at him. Sneering. He was tired, and hurt, and bewildered.

What was wrong? he asked himself again. Was he so clumsy, so personally objectionable, that his devotion meant nothing to Mary? Couldn't she understand that he would do anything he could, try anything, to please her, to make her happy? Was the whole trouble only that he wasn't a gentleman according to her definition of the word? But surely she was an intelligent person; she could see beyond surface veneer—or lack of it—to the real worth underneath! She could—if she wanted to. If—oh, if he could only understand women! What were they, what did they think, what did they want of a man and of life! Why wasn't a man's love, himself, enough?

Or was it all a game to them? A game for power, for advantage, a man's pawn against a woman's queen?

No, not with Mary. She was too honest. And yet, what other explanation would there be, unless it was just feminine perversity, which Mary, being a woman, could not entirely escape?

Back at the Tavern at last, Abe threw himself dejectedly across the bed (he never could lie straight in a bed, they were all too short), physically and emotionally exhausted, not knowing what to do next, nor even what he wanted to do.

Trying to figure it all out long after he should have been

sleeping, he could still only question himself: "Why are women such a profound wonder to me?"

Mary wasn't very happy that night, either.

As she walked home alone from the Mentor Grahams, she wondered why in the world she had treated Lincoln so. She hadn't wanted to be rude, had not intended to humiliate him. She wasn't in the habit of coquetry, let alone cruelty. For she knew quite well that Abe's crudeness was only a matter of training—or rather, lack of it—and had nothing whatever to do with his innate kindness or his mental ability. And that lack of training was not his fault, and couldn't be charged against him personally.

She tried to tell herself, in self-defense, that since he was capable of learning other things, he was also able to learn the rudiments of good breeding—if he were willing. That there was no hope for her of happiness with him unless he should learn.

But intuition told her that she might have goaded him too far this time. And she didn't want to end his courtship—yet. The trouble was, she couldn't make up her mind. There was so much to recommend him as a husband—brains, ambition, an amazing faculty for making friends, and an almost unlimited capacity for hard work, if he were interested. There was also something pathetically endearing about his clumsiness with women—his awkwardness in all the little tricks of compliments and attention. Nor was his honesty to be overlooked. Not only honesty in charging a fair price and paying a debt and giving an employer once-and-a-half the value of his wage. Honesty in words. Abe Lincoln would never say a thing he did not mean, that he would not stand by. He would never tell a woman he loved her unless he did. The greater difficulty was in trying to decide whether he loved her when he wouldn't tell!

So that all her mental arguing came back to one fact: that she wasn't ready to say yes, and she wasn't ready to say no to him. She needed more time, some particular incident, some definite speech or act of his, a real admission of love, to tip the scales and make her decision for her.

She certainly didn't want this quarrel to last. But how she'd get out of it and save her face, she had no idea.

She, too, was physically and mentally exhausted by the time she got home, and, even the bed she shared with the two Abell girls was welcome that night.

Chapter Twenty

"HAS ABE EVER COURTED A GIRL BEFORE?" MARY ASKED HER sister next morning. She was curious, for she wanted to settle in her own mind, once and for all, the recurring question as to the reason for his crudeness. If it was lack of experience rather than want of consideration, perhaps there was hope for him. A man couldn't be held guilty for lack of opportunity to learn. . . . . .

"Why, I hardly know," replied Betsey, wringing out the last of the baby diapers (which Mary had never offered to help her with), and calling out the door for one of the girls to come and hang them up to dry. She wiped her hands on her apron then, and sat down to knit while they talked. It was the fourth pair of mittens she'd made this fall, but she still had three pairs to go before the bad weather set in, to say nothing of her preparations for the new baby. The handdowns from one to another had worn out with constant use, and unless she got busy, the new child would live as naked as it arrived!

"I suppose he's had girl friends," she went on, "in spite of his looks, women have always liked Abe. I don't know that he's ever been serious about anyone. Unless," she added thoughtfully, "it was Ann."

"Who was Ann?"

"Oh, I thought you knew. Ann Rutledge. Jim's daughter. She died last year. Abe carried on pretty bad, but then everybody in the village took it hard. She was a lovely girl. Very sweet, and unassuming, and not at all spoiled by working in the Tavern. But she was engaged, for years, to John McNeil. He went east to get his family, and stayed for three years, and she stopped hearing from him. Folks said she just pined away. Then, soon after she died, he came back, but it was too late. The story is just like an English novel," she added as an afterthought. "But about Abe, he's so honest, and so decent, I don't believe he'd even think of seriously courting a girl who was engaged to another man. He just liked her, and felt bad when she died."

Mary had not heard of the account of the romance. One fact had filled her mind. "She worked in—in a tavern?" she asked, incredulous.

"She helped her father," returned Betsey with some asperity. "Jim Rutledge's place isn't a saloon, it's an inn. They had regular boarders there, very few travelers. Why, Abe lived there when you visited here before."

"Was Abe in love with her?" persisted Mary.

"I told you. Nobody ever knew. He might have been, if she'd been free. But she was promised to John McNeil. McNamar, his name really was. He changed it when he came out here."

Mary was mollified. Even if Abe had been in love with the tavernkeeper's daughter, the girl had been only an ordinary, pioneer child, who helped with the menial work about the place and had probably been totally uneducated. So, she concluded, Abe's blundering was due entirely to his lack of experience. Never having known a lady before, he just didn't know how to act. That made some difference.

"Betsey," she ventured hesitantly, but swallowing her pride at last, "we quarreled pretty badly before he went away. I reckon I fussed at him too much. And then last night . . . . would you be willing to ask him to come out, I mean, ask him specially, yourself?"

Betsey didn't think much of that idea. Mary had been wrong, she had been more inconsiderate than she'd ever accused Abe of being, and it was up to her to ask him to come back. But, after more argument, Betsey finally agreed, just because she saw no hope of patching up the stubborn romance in any other way. Somebody in this crazy business had to use some sense.

It was almost time for Abe Lincoln to return to Vandalia. He was keenly interested in this session of the legislature. For now he knew the ropes; he had served his apprenticeship. He was through listening, and ready to speak up when it came his turn.

At last, some action was going to be taken toward the establishment of a permanent state capital. With the new influx of settlers from the East into the northern part of the state, Vandalia was no longer the center of population. At the same time, the roads and transportation were not improving in proportion to the demands made upon them, and it became increasingly difficult for members to get to and from Vandalia. The booming state of Illinois needed a new capital, one which would be easily accessible to all of its legislators, one nearer to the center of the state. Proposals for the moving of the capital were to come before the legislature this session.

Abe wanted the permanent capital to be located at Springfield, in his own county. And he was ready to move heaven and earth and a couple of committees to do it. The benefit to Springfield and to the county would be immeasurable. New residents, new money, new ideas would create a boom in Springfield which nothing else short of a gold mine could produce, to say nothing of the standing the town would gain throughout the state.

Abe saw, too, his opportunity for personal success in the battle for the new location. If he could put that over, he was made with his own constituency, and moreover, the whole legislative body would recognize him as a serious protagonist.

He had it all figured out, too. Every constituency in the state was after appropriations for internal improvements. Every county wanted a road, a bridge, a drainage canal, or something that could be financed by state money. But Sangamon County wanted the state capital. The Sangamon delegation—eight tall men besides himself, so nearly of a size that they were already being called the "Long Nine"— looked to him as their leader and would vote with him as one man. A little trading here, a little support there from the Long Nine, and the other counties would get their roads —and Springfield would become the capital. It would be as easy as that. With a little luck thrown in.

He was ready for it, eager for it, and already his mind had arrived in Vandalia and had gone to work. The last few days in New Salem, he felt disembodied, as one in a nightmare who looks across the room and sees himself sitting over there in the corner, both observer and observed. It was uncanny. Here he was in New Salem, but he wasn't here at all. He was a man in a dream, an automaton, making motions.

There was that matter of unfinished business to attend to before he left. That unsettled question with Mary. He had work to do in Vandalia, and he didn't want any emotional uncertainties nagging at his mind, distracting his attention. He wanted the thing settled, one way or the other. The woman would simply have to make up her mind.

Why am I so perverse when I'm with him? Mary thought desperately as she listened with half an ear to Abe's predictions of the coming battles in the legislature. When he's away, I weigh his good qualities against his bad ones, and I have sense enough to recognize that his faults are superficial, and that his mind and his character more than make up for them. Then when I see him, he rubs me all the wrong way! I get my arguments piled up in neat stacks, and decide reasonably that he'd make a fine husband in spite of everything, and then he comes to see me, and I'm no more certain than I was the last time he was here! Why can't I decide? It isn't fair to him not to!

She was really pleased with the interest he took in his work. When he talked of the political world and his growing place in it, his ugly face lit up until there was a kind of beauty in it—it became alive and eager, and the rough lines softened. His speech was improving too, she thought. He was beginning to get the feel of an audience. A kind of dramatic quality colored his simplest statements. Yes, he was surely growing, his personality taking on bolder, surer outlines.

But still she couldn't answer his inevitable question.

When he had finished describing to her a midget-sized lawyer from Jacksonville, named Douglas, whom he reckoned "the least man I've ever seen" but one with a good deal of fireworks in his nature, Mary knew he was about talked out, and she guessed what was coming next. And she was no nearer an answer than she'd ever been. She was also very unhappy about it.

So when he stopped for breath and said, "Now, Mary, about us," she tried to be gentle, as kind as she knew how to be.

All she could say, surely, was, "Abe, why don't you just forget that you've formally proposed to me, and go to Vandalia and your work, free? I'm just not certain—yet. Marriage is such a definite, finished, desperate affair, and it's so terribly important to a woman, that I can't go into it without being sure. I admire you so very much, Abe, and I'm frightfully fond of you. You've no idea how I'll miss you. But I'm afraid I haven't fallen in love with you."

"What is 'falling in love,' Mary?" he asked. "How would you ever know?"

"All I know," she replied, "is that if a girl is in love, she doesn't question. She knows. So, as long as I have any doubt at all, well, I'm just not in love."

The divine fire, the great ecstasy, the thing the poets rhymed about? If that was what she wanted, would she—could she—ever find it in him? he questioned himself bitterly. And if that was love, if the poetic flame was a human experience and not the creation of imaginative rhymers, it had surely never happened to him. Whether it ever would, he doubted. For man's frame can house only one mighty conflagration, and his was ambition. He knew that now. He had offered this woman what he had to give, and more no man could tender. Yet, he must care, in his own way, for he wasn't willing to give up. It was more than just a matter of a bargain with her sister. He wanted to marry this girl, if only he could be sure of pleasing her and making her happy.

"Mary," he urged, "I must have some definite understanding with you, soon. Perhaps you'll be able to think more clearly about it after I've gone. Will you write me so that I may have your letters soon after I reach Vandalia?"

His face and his voice were so pleading, and the few days' respite he offered so attractive, that Mary had to promise. He might be right. When he had gone, perhaps she could straighten out her thoughts. She knew quite well that she owed him her answer, if only for courtesy's sake. And maybe—maybe something would happen to help her decide, to sway her judgment one way or the other.

"Yes, Abe, I'll write you," she promised. "Soon. You can depend on that."

He seemed happier, calmer, when he said goodnight and started back over the familiar way to the village. Yet there was something pathetic about the long, patient stride of the man. She had treated him abominably, and she knew it.

"Oh Lord," she thought, "help me to decide! Help me to make up my mind soon!"

But her thoughts were in greater confusion than ever, and she hadn't much hope.

Chapter Twenty One

*I*T WAS LIKE THE OPENING MOVEMENTS OF A CHECKER GAME, thought Abe the first day of the December session. Routine motions filled the day; the election of a speaker, a door-keeper, unimportant details taking up important time, while each coterie measured the strength of its opponents and figured out its own plan of action.

Familiar to Abe now were the rippling undercurrents of excitement, the pull of urgency against the need for caution and wariness, the necessity of estimating to the last fraction of an ounce the weight of one's adversaries. The need for perfect timing, for patience. Play both ends against the middle: one delegation's greed or downright necessity against another's civic pride; and then if you're lucky, if you play it without depending on luck and the luck comes along to help just a little bit, you'll get what you want. You'll get the capital moved to Springfield. We need roads and bridges and canals, and God knows what we don't need in Sangamon County, but we need the capital more than anything. If we get the capital, the other things will come.

It would be a slow game, and a long one, and nothing

could be done at all until after the Governor's address, which was scheduled for Friday.

In the interim, Abe had time to think about Mary Owens.

She had promised to write to him, but day followed day without word from her. Between his impatience for a letter, the inactivity in the House, and general fatigue, Abe fell into one of those brooding black spells of melancholy, when life itself seemed too difficult to sustain.

He had hoped that, back here in Vandalia, in his own world (it was a long way back to New Salem, not only in miles, but in the distance that he had traveled since first leaving the village!) he would be able to see his strange love affair in better proportion, with some kind of perspective. Perhaps he wouldn't even want to marry Mary then!

Searching his motives now, he suspected that his courtship had been impelled more by pride than by interest. Granted that Mary had been a congenial mental companion (when she wasn't fussing at him), and that he could do much worse than marry her, the gist of it was that the woman's vacillation attacked his self-esteem until she became a challenge, a "double-dare" that he could not ignore, and it was necessary to his ego to get a "yes" out of her, whether he actually wanted it or not. Somehow, he had to convince her that Abe Lincoln would be a good catch, even for Squire Owens' daughter.

As time frittered away and there was no letter from her—she had said, "You can depend on it!"—he decided that he must again take the initiative, and at least remind her of his existence.

Already the politician who must weigh every statement

to which he signed his name, Abe labored slowly over the letter, and then, after several bad starts, hit on what he thought was just the right mixture of personalities and general information. By now, the governor had made his opening speech, Taylor had delivered his petition for a new county, there'd been an Internal Improvement Convention. Things were lining up, and he had something to tell her. She had always been interested in politics. In fact, they'd had their best talks when he was telling her about the doings in the House.

But he told her, too, that he had been unwell, for it was true, and he had always found her sympathetic. ". . . . that, with other things I can not account for . . . ." she might, if she liked, attribute her silence as one of the things! "have conspired and have gotten my spirits so low, that I feel I would rather be any place in the world than here. . . . . Write back as soon as you get this, and if possible, say something that will please me, for really I have not been pleased since I left you." That ought to do it! That ought to prove his feeling for her (even though he wasn't sure of it himself!) without laying his pride too wide open to hurt. At the very worst, the letter would remind her of him, perhaps goad her to answer.

Reading it over after he had finished it—it was a mighty long letter—Abe found that he had said nothing he really wanted to write, and what he had said he'd done badly. He was too tired to start over. Surely, she would understand. If she didn't, it was still the best he could do. He posted the letter, and tried to compose himself to wait.

Bennett Abell came home from the village so much disturbed that he didn't even ask Mary for news of Abe's doings in the letter he had brought her. He had news of his own.

"The town seems to be fallin' apart," he told the women, "nobody's interested in the church, or the clubs, or the doin's any more, and all you hear is talk of better land somewhere yonder. Ever since the 'Utility' grounded, they've been gittin' an itchin' foot, one after another. And Taylor, settin' up over in Petersburg. Even the drunkards are leavin'."

Betsey crumbled her cornbread, thoughtfully. "The village didn't lose anything when it lost Doc Regnier and Jack Kelso." Discouragement had set in when the boat "Utility" floundered, and the settlement had to admit at last that the river wasn't navigable. The settlers, she and Bennett among them, had dreamed great dreams of the development of the region, and the hopes had been pinned to the false promise of the Sangamon. No town can grow, and become great, if it can't move goods in and out.

But that wasn't all of it, Betsey reflected. It was more as if the motive force of the town had gone, the one personality that gave it excuse for living. It had served its purpose, and now the village had no reason to struggle on.

"It isn't the river alone, Bennett," she told him. "It just seems as if Abe held the town together. He sort of kept folks going, and kept them interested, and—and contented. If he'd settled here, they wouldn't have got that itch in their feet."

Bennett thought it was just like a woman to find sentimental rather than practical reasons for the town's disintegration. New Salem was dying. There was no future here, not even for a farmer. Not for a man who, albeit he was approaching middle age, had not many years ago dreamed of building an empire in the West. Bennett doubted if he'd find what he wanted as close by as Petersburg, Jacksonville, or Beardstown.

"They say Missouri's a right fertile country," he offered, and a far-away look crept into his eyes, the look that Betsey had seen fifteen years ago, when he was courting her, and talking of Illinois. To move, to pull up their roots and trek over the country again, to a new wilderness, forsaking all they had built here, to start over, no longer young, with half of their working years behind them . . . . .

"I wonder if he'll ever come back to stay?" she mused aloud, even while she knew the answer.

"Who?" asked Bennett, his thoughts in Missouri. "Your brother Sam?" Sam Owens had gone out to Missouri several years ago, and though he didn't write often, the family judged he was doing well.

"Why Abe, of course. He could put new life into New Salem. He could save it."

"He couldn't open up the river," replied Bennett doggedly. A town had to have transportation. It had to get its goods out, and necessities in. Petersburg might live and it might not, but Chicago was booming because it crouched on the shore of Lake Michigan.

Missouri, on the other side of the Mississippi, with access to the Gulf and the sea, should be a better place than any for a man with empiric ideas. There was no false promise in the Mississippi. It rushed on turbulently to the Gulf, and commerce flowed with it, surely and without mishap, to the rich market of New Orleans. Abe Lincoln couldn't save it. Nothing could save it.

"No, Betsey," he told her, "Abe won't be back to stay. He never had his feet stuck to the ground."

In her heart, Betsey knew that he was right. Abe had no feel for the land, no longing for possession or property, no inclination for business. His place was in the world of men and ideas, not with the plows and the mill wheels. Already he had begun, he had shown what he could do, and all she could sincerely feel for him was happiness in his growing success, and an aching nostalgia for the old days of comradeship when, easy and even a little lazy, not yet dogged by any definite ambition, he had sat at her board and told her the light news of the day. Those times were gone, as their youth was gone, and he had his eyes set on some far place that none of them could see. He'd reach that place—but she snapped back abruptly to the present problem of her unmanageable sister. Would Mary Owens have horse sense enough to be at his side when he got there?

Mary had paid little attention to the talk at dinner. She had been re-reading in her mind that strange letter from Abe.

For a man who had so urgently pressed his demand for marriage before he left, it certainly wasn't what you could call a love letter!

Grant that he still didn't know where he stood with her, and that she had failed to keep her solemn promise of writing to him—and that only because she hadn't known what to say—still, a two-page letter filled with nothing but political talk and complaints of his health wouldn't help her much to make up her mind.

She was dismayed, as she had been since the beginning of his courtship, by his lack of warmth, the absence of any indication that he cared for her. He had said everything except what she wanted him to say. He had written of his health, which of course would concern any woman who was interested in him, of his growing importance as a Representative, and the promise of success in his activities. He hadn't told her that he loved her. That was the only thing that she wanted to know.

Well, in all decency, she'd have to answer his letter. She'd answer him in kind. He'd get back the same sort of inane letter he had written. How else could she write?

When she came to write him, she told him of the unrest in New Salem, of Bennett's yearning for Missouri, the small talk of their neighbors, and expressed her sincere concern for his health. Why were they trying to hold sessions of the Legislature in the unfinished, unheated building which Vandalia was pushing up too rapidly in the hope of retaining the capital there? It was a wonder they didn't all die from exposure!

That was the best she could do. She still needed time—time or some deciding circumstance—to enable her to give him a definite answer. Moreover, she thought in some pique, in his own letter he hadn't asked for an answer to his oft-repeated question. Let him stew a while longer. . . . .

Chapter Twenty Two

$\mathcal{B}$Y THE TIME MARY'S REPLY REACHED ABE, THE LEGISLATURE was getting into full swing, and he could indulge in only momentary disappointment and anger at the commonplace and indefinite quality of her letter.

Douglas—he whom Abe had described to Mary as "the least man I've even seen"—had brought in from the Committee on Petitions a bill for the formation of a new county out of a portion of Sangamon. The proposed county seemed to Abe ridiculously small in area to constitute a political entity, so he jumped into the fracas, glad of action at last. Getting himself onto a select committee with Wilson of his own county and Richardson of Schuyler, he decided at last to throw his weight for acceptance of a compromise bill, even though acceptance could hardly be expected. But the debate was good. He was getting into things again, making himself heard, not letting them forget him. He was building up to the big fight for the relocation of the capital, and every small triumph helped.

The creation of the new county was a major issue. For if the representation of Sangamon County was cut, they might not pass the Seat-of-Government Bill. When, just before

Christmas, proposals for the system of internal improvements were brought up, the plots and counter-plots thickened, and the real drama began to develop.

Abe was really interested in the improvements, and when a petition came up to change the state road which ran by John McNeil's farm, out in the Sand Ridge neighborhood northwest of New Salem, it seemed like he owed it to John to let him know, and advise his friend that if he didn't want the road changed, he'd better stir himself to protest.

All the time, though, Abe was chafing against the delay, the waiting, the leading up to the big fight. The death and funeral of Resolve Graham, from Gallatin, with the resultant recess and inaction following right after the Christmas holiday, were more minor irritations.

He had little time to think about Mary Owens. When he did think of her, she was only a nagging bit of unfinished business, that teased his pride—a problem that must be taken care of when his important work was completed. He had no need right now for letters that would "please" him. He was almighty well pleased with himself.

Slowly, like the slowed-down motions in a dream, the internal improvement bill—that legislation which was to saddle the state with an eight-million-dollar debt in spite of nation-wide indications of panic—was shaping up. They propped up the wobbling State Bank with two million dollars' worth of stock, and congratulated themselves on their foresightedness, Abe Lincoln along with the rest. What better way was there to use the taxpayers' money than in stabilizing their own Bank? Prosperity was here to stay.

It was hey-day in the Legislature, and Abe Lincoln was having the time of his life.

After the tension of the day, there was nothing much to do except gather around at one another's living quarters and look over the day's spoils and plan the next maneuver.

Abe found that these fellows—Senators and Representatives—some of them substantial businessmen, some established lawyers, some seasoned politicians, were just about the same kind of folks as those he'd left behind in New Salem.

He dug out some of his old stories, and his colleagues laughed just as hard, sitting about a fancy hotel lobby, as Henry Onstot and Denton Offutt had, straddling upturned whiskey kegs back in the old store.

Good black cigars—though he never smoked them; sometimes liquor fumes—though he never drank; and good talk and good fellowship. Men who thought in terms of two million dollars for the Bank instead of two bushels of corn. Men who were concerned with the election of a state senator rather than a local justice of the peace. But they were the same kind of people he had known so well in New Salem. They wanted the same things out of life—success and security, and a little fun as they went along. They liked the same kind of jokes.

Abe told them about the Sangamon River boat with the five-foot boiler and the seven-foot whistle, and the horse he'd ridden in the Indian War that had once belonged to an undertaker who had sold it because it couldn't get the corpse to the cemetery in time for the resurrection; he told them how his father had grubbed hazelnut bushes back in Indiana so that the farm wouldn't know it was for sale.

But it was pretty Eliza Browning, wife of Orville Browning from Quincy, who stimulated him to his brightest sallies.

Browning, being a member of the Senate, was not involved in the Sangamon delegation's intrigues in the House, but he was sympathetic to their desire to make Springfield the capital of the state, and he promised Abe full support for the project when the question came to the upper house.

Browning liked Abe Lincoln. He liked him so much that he introduced the Whig leader of the lower house to his wife.

Abe's confidence was running so high that he was not embarrassed when he met the Senator's lovely wife. In fact, he was so much at ease that she discovered quite readily what her husband had seen in the sprouting politician who, in spite of his obvious growing pains, had almost reached his height and needed only to fill out a little to become a real power in the state.

Eliza Browning's charm and quick sympathy drew him out without his realizing it.

"I understand, Mr. Lincoln," she told him, "that you are from Kentucky, too."

"Yes ma'am," he replied seriously, "but not your part of Kentucky."

He was so unassuming and genuine that they became friends at once.

This was a new kind of woman, different from any Abe had ever known. As comfortable as Betsey Abell, but as polished as though she'd spent her whole life in the courts of Europe. Friendly and sympathetic and understanding, without the critical attitude which had made his friendship with Mary so difficult.

She knew politics, too. She listened by the hour to her husband's and Abe's accounts of the by-play of wits in the Legislature, and she laughed with them or became serious or angry with them, as the case warranted.

Mary Owens was not a woman like this, he reflected. Compared with Mrs. Browning, she was provincial and limited in her outlook, in spite of her education. And she had none of Eliza Browning's tolerance or warmth in friendship.

Moreover, Orville Browning's wife was safely married, and there was no question of his friendship for her being misunderstood. . . . .

Through a mass of detail that you couldn't stir with a stick, the Legislature plodded on until at last, early in February, the first move toward the relocation of the capital was made, in an attempt to repeal the Act of 1833 designed to locate permanently the seat of the state government.

That Act had to be disposed of first, and Abe led the move for its repeal. He could show his hand now, for the drama was in the last act. No need for diplomacy any longer—the excitement was on.

That excitement lasted a long time. Day after day annoying by-plays were introduced, with the Fayette County (Vandalia) contingent trying to table the bill every time their position got shaky. First they tried to put it over to December, 1839; failing that, they attempted to set it aside and organize a board of seven commissioners to ascertain the exact geographical center of the state. Defeated again, another bunch of partisans tried to table the bill until July fourth. That was on a Saturday, and Abe pushed through a motion to table the bill only until Monday, and also wore down a countermove to submit the whole thing to the people.

It wasn't until the following Friday that, by a circumlocutionary process worthy of a bird dog stalking its prey, he was able to force the bill to issue, and he pounded through an amendment providing that the General Assembly reserve the right to repeal the new Act at any later date it pleased. That was putting sugar on the pill which was apparently so distasteful to everyone but the members of the Sangamon delegation.

On Saturday, February 25, the Senate reported (thank heaven for Orville Browning!) its approval of the bill providing for a permanent location of the capital, and Abe knew it was all over but the shouting. All over, that was, except the actual selection of the site, and Abe knew that, if his friends kept their commitments as he had kept his through all the crazy balancing and counter-balancing, Springfield would win.

Can you take a man's word when spoils are at stake? Would some of his pledges, gained through friendship and mutual benefit, be bought off at the last minute? He couldn't tell. A man can only plug up every leak he can see, and pray that there aren't any he can't see, or that his worst adversary will break a leg the night before the final voting.

All of Monday the House fooled around with petty discussion and parliamentary motions, while the tension grew and half the members began to wonder if they'd get home by spring. Monday the twenty-seventh was the day the House had set for adjournment. Everyone was restive, tired of discussion, tired of chasing one another around Robin Hood's barn.

By Tuesday even the diehards were ready to vote. And Springfield won on the fourth ballot.

The struggle, the excitement, the fun, were over. And Abe Lincoln's name was made in the Legislature. He'd done it—he'd killed the bear. Now he could go back to New Salem with real spoils!

Chapter Twenty Three

ON THE WAY BACK TO NEW SALEM, ABE BEGAN TO THINK OF
Mary again.

It seemed to him she should be right well pleased with
what he would be able to tell her. Not only with his bagging
the capital for Springfield, but with that last piece of diplomacy which he had saved until after the final vote on the
capital.

That was his formal protest, along with Dan Stone, against
the anti-abolitionist resolutions of January. While the capital
bill was pending, he and his colleague from Sangamon
hadn't dared protest against those resolutions, for fear of
antagonizing members whose support they needed for their
pet project. But now they could come out from behind their
bush and say what they thought.

The Illinois resolutions, following the pattern of those of
Virginia, Kentucky, Alabama, Connecticut, and New York,
Abe felt, were wrong. Illinois' formal stand on the question
that was inflaming the country—with William Lloyd Garrison down east pouring coal-oil on the fire every time it
began to die down—was purely legal. The Illinois House
had declared that Congress has the right to deal with slavery

in the District of Columbia and nowhere else, and let it go at that, and went blithely on to pass a resolution to encourage the killing of wolves, as though both considerations fell within the same category.

Well, thought Abe, and Dan Stone agreed with him, the legal issue was only a small part of it. The trouble was that the eastern abolitionists were, by their misunderstanding and their violence, stirring up antagonism and panic in the South until already they had undone the good that had been accomplished over years toward the gradual betterment of the slaves.

Slavery he hated. Human bondage in any form, for black or white, had no place in a Christian nation. But the way of Garrison and his followers was stirring up dissension that might easily get out of hand and do more harm than good. The way toward any improvement, political, economic, or social, was through understanding and education, not through hatred and violence.

So the protest, his and Stone's, spread on the House Journal their belief that slavery is bad, but that the "promulgation of abolition doctrines tends rather to increase than abate the evils of slavery."

Mary should be pleased with that. He had never discussed slavery with her much, but he knew how she felt about it. She had grown up with slaves, and her father's attitude was one of benevolent paternalism. Mary would hate the abolitionists. And she would commend Abe's insight, and his open declaration.

She would be pleased with a lot of things he'd done. Returning to New Salem as the acknowledged Whig leader in the House, with a record of real accomplishment behind him and a new assurance in his thought and in his speech, he was not the floundering blunderbuss who had humbly urged his suit last November. He was a seasoned politician, with a few laurels in his crown, and Eliza Browning's friendship had made him feel that personally he was at least not a monstrosity.

And he had been admitted to the Illinois Bar just before the close of the Legislative Session—in fact, the day after his victory on the capital location bill. Not only that, but Major John T. Stuart, whom he had known in the Indian War, the same Stuart who had first advised him to read law, had asked him to come to Springfield as a partner in his own law office.

There was no future for a lawyer in New Salem. Abe was beginning to have his doubts of anyone's future there from what he had heard. But Springfield, with the new capital in sight, and partnership with a man of Stuart's caliber, was an open door to so much opportunity that even he couldn't gauge it.

Abe had something to offer Mary now. And with his confidence and pride restored by the winter in Vandalia, he was sure that this time her answer would be yes. Surely, she could find no reason for hedging any longer.

As he made the long journey back to the village his dreams were rosy, glowing with promise of success and happiness, bright with hope.

And yet, the dreams were edged with nostalgia. For this return to New Salem was only a visit, a brief re-acquaintance with a part of his life that was done, that he had had to cast off like an outgrown coat, even while he remembered its warm comfort. The lazy, carefree days were gone. The loafing days, when he had been nagged by indecision, but when there was still time to decide. The long, sunny hours, sitting on the river bank with Jack Kelso, while Jack fished or only talked; and there was the beauty of the water, and the beauty of the words Jack knew, the poetry that sang like the sparkling river. The good talk; the yarning in the stores, the taverns, the mill, when men came in to pass the time of day and sit in judgment on cabbages and kings. They generally ended up listening to the stories he'd picked up here and yonder, or asking his advice and opinion on the current political issues. Oh, he'd been a big toad-frog in a little puddle in New Salem, back in that time before ambition began to ride him, when every day had been sufficient, and he hadn't known where his next meal was to come from.

But the meals had always come, sometimes scanty, sometimes prodigal, and his ambition had crystallized. He could no longer deny it.

New Salem was a part of his life to which he could return now only for respite, for he had found his road, and the signposts all pointed away. But he loved every tree, every ditch and gulley, every turn and caprice of the bright Sangamon, every house and cabin, man, woman, child, and dog in the village. Saying goodbye to New Salem was saying goodbye to part of himself, a person that he had been and could be no longer.

Well, for a day or two he could come back. Get into that old self, and wander over the hillside, loaf along the stream, and talk mighty talk in the stores and in the taverns.

Spring was creeping over the March fields, and there might be snowflowers hidden in the woods, that he could search for with Mary Owens. . . . .

Abe's fame had reached New Salem ahead of him, and his old cronies—what few there were left—had gathered in the village for his arrival. Sam Hill and Henry Onstot, and a few of the Clary's Grove boys greeted him at Hill's store.

The little store that had once been crowded with boisterous farmers and tradesmen seemed larger than it had before, and the corner where Abe had kept the paraphernalia of the post office was curiously empty. Hill's stock was depleted, too, reduced to the barest essentials—coffee and salt and tobacco, and of course, whiskey. That would be wanted as long as there was one man left in town.

The bright spring sun betrayed mercilessly the growing shabbiness of the whole town, an abandoned building here, a broken fence there, doors flapping on broken hinges.

"It's going, Abe," Onstot told him. "There's nothing can save the town. It was the river. The river let us down. Even an act of legislature couldn't save it. It would take an act of God."

"To make the river run uphill?" asked Abe drily, but the disintegration of his village saddened him. Somehow, although he had known it couldn't be, he had hoped that he would find New Salem the same, a part of his youth standing still, not changing, to be there whenever he could return. "I reckon you're right, Henry," he added. "It was the river done us wrong."

"That fool river," put in Hill, "isn't worth a tinker's dam

except to look at! Even Jack Kelso got sick of fishin' in the thing, and moved on!"

"I know. Where did he go?" Abe felt a sharp longing for his old friend. If only Jack were here, things would be almost the same.

"Just wandered off without sayin' boo to anybody. Some say he struck out for Missouri. We'll all be goin' soon. Can't sit up with a corpse forever. There's no life here any more."

"I guess not." Nothing here. Nothing but his youth, his long, lazy dreams. His youth that was gone, replaced by maturity. Dead youth, dead dreams, dead town. And you couldn't sit up with a corpse forever.

But now his friends wanted to know about the Legislature, about the "Seat of Government Bill."

"How did you put it over, Abe? How in tarnation did you buck all those moneyed men and city slickers?" They knew Abe could do anything he set out to do in politics, but they wanted a play-by-play account, a detailing of the battle, an understanding of the machinery of political maneuvering. Their own dreams fading, they wanted to bask in Abe's glory, to feel that they had a stake in his success because he was one of them.

So he told them all about it, the little bills he had supported to gain votes for his own, the men he had cultivated to help his project, and the men who couldn't be cultivated and had to be fought. He colored it all up with his dry humor, and made it live for them as it had for him, so that they could share the drama with him. He didn't forget, either, to tell them how the Sangamon delegation, the Long

Nine, had pulled together like one man, inseparable, a bloc that couldn't be beaten.

Then he told them, after his bill was passed, he and Stone had gone on the record in their protest against the anti-abolitionist resolutions. "We couldn't do a thing till after the bill was passed," he explained. "We didn't dare to. There are too many conflicting sympathies in Illinois, and we couldn't risk getting somebody mad at us who might otherwise vote for Springfield. But we got ourselves heard, just before the Legislature adjourned. It's a bad thing for the country, this bitterness over slavery. It's almost as bad as the slavery, for hatred makes men lose their sense of proportion. A thing as bad as slavery takes tolerance and understanding to cure it, not violence."

They agreed with him, but they saw that Abe's interests were outgrowing them, leaping beyond local considerations to national issues, to economic and moral problems which so far had never touched New Salem. They forced him back to their own urgent concern, just to get onto solid ground again.

"It's a mighty fine thing, getting the capital at Springfield. It'll help the county. But it won't save New Salem."

He assented. Prosperity for Springfield wouldn't help New Salem. New Salem was a bubble that had burst, and you couldn't pick up the vapor in your hands and make a bubble out of it again.

"What you goin' to do now?" Hill asked him.

Abe knew what Sam meant. He didn't mean right now, this minute. He meant in the near future. For everybody knew that a man couldn't just live off of grass between sessions of the Legislature—or live very long on what he made as a Representative. But Abe begged the issue, for somehow, he didn't want to tell his friends right now that he was going to follow—or anticipate—prosperity in Springfield.

"Why, I think I'll mosey out to see Bennett and Betsey," he replied. "I can never stay long in New Salem without I land up out there."

That allowed no argument, but after he had loped down the road, Henry speculated, "Wonder if she'll say yes this time? He's sure got something to offer her now."

"She'll never marry him," replied Sam Hill. "My wife is her best friend—grew up together—and Parthena knows her pretty well. Mary Owens will never hitch up to the likes of him, politics or no politics. He's not her kind."

"She might like the governor's mansion. And Abe won't be poor forever."

"No, he won't be poor all his life. He'll make money, and he'll get to a high position. But she wants something Abe can never get."

They watched his ungainly figure that now had a sort of ugly dignity about it, until he was out of sight down the road, and then they went back into the store. The March wind was raw, in spite of the bright spring sunshine.

Out at the Abells', Abe's friends had literally killed the fatted calf for his return.

He was greeted like a long-lost relative, or a conquering hero, or both.

And here, at least, everything was the same. The farm was well cared for, and looked prosperous. He went with

Bennett about the place, inspecting the livestock, praising the improvements. Perhaps the unrest of the village hadn't got this far, in spite of what Mary had written him. Maybe Bennett would find some other market for his goods, be able to take it over to Petersburg or Beardstown, and so stay on. Bennett wasn't a boom-town follower, he was a farmer. If only this place, these friends, remain the same, Abe thought, I'll have a place to come back to, a little spot where I can relax from strain, and be myself. Maybe Bennett will stay. . . . .

Back in the house, both Betsey and Mary made a great fuss over him, and he lined the children up in mock solemnity so that he could count their noses and learn if there were any new ones since he'd left.

Then the Abells too must hear of all his shenanigans in the Legislature, and he went through the whole story again, and told them about his protest against the anti-abolitionist resolutions, watching Mary for her reaction as he talked, eager for her approval.

But she made no comment, and so he went on to explain his decision to settle in Springfield, and to add his name to John Stuart's shingle.

Mary's face lit up then. "Why, Abe, that's wonderful!" she exclaimed. "Mr. Stuart is a fine lawyer, and starting your practice with him will be splendid experience and training!"

Her words, "experience and training," told him that she knew he wouldn't stop with a small law practice in Springfield, but would go on and on.

He wanted to see her alone now, to paint even more glowingly for her his chances of success, and to have from her at last her promise to share it with him.

Betsey seemed to have the same idea, for she shooed her reluctant husband out of the house, and found something to do herself in another room.

Abe and Mary were alone, at last, and she looked happier than he'd seen her in a long time. She repeated, "It's perfectly wonderful, your going to Springfield to practice law!"

That seemed more important to her than his success in the Legislature, but he guessed it was natural in a woman. Politics can shift and change, and the man who is in the limelight today can be totally eclipsed tomorrow, but a good law practice is something you can tie to.

"I'm pleased about it," he admitted. "You know it was John Stuart advised me to read law in the first place, 'way back there when we were chasing Black Hawk."

"Yes, you told me." She seemed to be waiting, and he reckoned it was time now to remind her that his offer of marriage was still good.

"Have you decided, Mary, whether you want to take a chance with me?" he asked.

Looking at him so full of enthusiasm and bright prospects, she felt the nagging doubt in her heart almost stilled. He would succeed. Mary knew that now. He would go far, almost as far as Betsey was always predicting he would. His wife would go with him. If only he'd say that he loved her, that she could contribute something personally to his success—or even that he needed her. If he'd say or do anything besides just sit there and practically reiterate that he was an honorable man and would stick by his word! If she only really knew that he wanted to marry her!

"Abe," she said, talking rapidly to get it over, "you're just about to start practicing law. Go down to Springfield and get on your feet, get established, and then—" she didn't finish because she couldn't. She wasn't ready, even yet, to say yes.

But he took her enthusiasm for yes. "I'll do that, Mary," he promised. "I'll do it. And you'll write to me?"

"Of course. Let me know how it goes, all about everything. Even your cases!"

He made a comical face. "Perhaps you're over-optimistic when you anticipate my cases," he said, and the tension was relieved by his humor.

However, saying goodbye to her, he was mightily encouraged. She had practically promised to marry him. And her delay had avoided for him the necessity of telling her that he had hardly a dollar to his name. . . . .

Chapter Twenty Four

*M*UD WAS ANKLE DEEP IN THE STREETS OF SPRINGFIELD when Abe rode into town on a borrowed horse. It was the 15th of April, and the spring rains had not spared the city of his future fortune. The horse was tired from its journey, and so was Abe. The only difference was that Abe had to worry about bed and board, and the horse didn't.

He was acquainted with Springfield, from his many visits, and the smartest thing to do about the problem of living quarters, he argued, would be to buy himself a bed and bed-clothes, and then find an unfurnished room. That would be cheaper, in the long run, than furnished lodgings. But what would he use for money? He hadn't a thing in the world but his prospects, and when he tried to translate them into concrete, worldly things, they appeared no more substantial than the bright bubbles of daydreams. At least, they wouldn't buy much.

Well, he'd have to run some credit, some way. This wasn't New Salem, where he could always make out, but the least he could do was try.

He hunted up a cabinetmaker and arranged to have a bed made to fit his unusual length. If he had to buy a bed, by jing, he was going to have one that he wouldn't have to sleep in doubled up as if he had the cramps!

Now for bedclothes—well, maybe his luck would hold. He wandered into the store run by that new young Kentuckian, Speed, toting his saddlebags with him.

"What would be your price," he asked the handsome young proprietor, "for bedclothes for a single bed—sheets, pillowcase, blankets and coverlid?"

Joshua Speed added quickly in his head. "Seventeen dollars, more or less."

Abe sighed. "It is cheap enough," he said, "but I can't pay it. If you will credit me till Christmas, I'll pay then—if I do well. If I don't, I may never be able to pay you."

Speed looked into the gloomy face of the tall stranger, and seemed satisfied with what he saw there.

"I have a large room with a double bed which you are welcome to share with me," he offered thoughtfully.

"Where is your room?"

"Upstairs," Speed replied, pointing to a winding stair that led up from the store.

Without a word, Abe picked up his saddlebags, carried them upstairs, and then raced joyfully down, taking three steps at a time.

"Well, Speed, I'm moved!" he rejoiced.

The world was suddenly bright again. . . . .

There was so much to do. He had to report to Stuart right away. The law office which he was to share was above the room in which the Circuit Court met, when in session, and, splendid lawyer though John Stuart was, his workshop was a pretty poor makeshift. Small, badly kept, containing nothing but bare essentials in the way of furnishings, it looked anything but prosperous. Stuart didn't have many books, either. He practiced law mostly from his head.

The first thing Stuart did after greeting his new partner was show him the announcement that had appeared in a local paper that very day, following formal notice of the dissolution of the partnership of John Stuart and Henry E. Dummer:

> "John T. Stuart and A. Lincoln
> Attorneys and Counsellors at Law,
> will practice, conjointly, in the Courts
> of this Judicial Circuit.
> Office No. 4, Hoffman's Row, upstairs.
> Springfield, April 12, 1837."

It was a mighty fine announcement. Abe reckoned it made him a full-fledged lawyer, at last.

William Butler, clerk of the Circuit Court and a friend of Stuart's, took Abe home with him that night to supper, and in a burst of friendliness, suggested that he continue to board there.

Abe's immediate difficulties were solved, almost as easily as they'd been taken care of back in New Salem. All he had to do now was sit back and wait for clients. . . . .

Springfield was as far removed from Vandalia as the old state capital was from New Salem.

There were as many as fifteen hundred people here, and the town had got over its growing pains, and was becoming a flourishing city. Round and about the Court House Square, in the center of town, clustered nineteen drygoods stores, one wholesale and six retail groceries, four drugstores, and, wonder and joy, a bookstore. There were four hotels, and Abe speculated with satisfaction that there would be ample accommodation for the members of the Legislature when they were finally moved to Springfield. The town boasted eighteen doctors—one for less than every hundred of population—and almost as many lawyers. Springfield was well bulwarked for any kind of human trouble, physical or legal.

But Abe wondered idly if the six churches, each with a resident minister, kept the folks any holier than the average run of human beings, and he reckoned there'd be just as much litigation here per capita as in hamlets less girded against the devil.

Yes, the new capital was different from New Salem, to which he had come, six years ago, penniless and ignorant of all occupations except those involving physical toil. He was still penniless, but thank God or Abe Lincoln or his friends—or all of them—he wasn't as ignorant as he'd been then! He had learned surveying and the law, and the ways of politics and men in high places. He had learned that his wits were a match for other men's experience; that he, with nothing behind him except log-cabin privation and the lessons learned by hardship, was an adversary for the best of them.

Wandering about the streets of Springfield, partly to kill time and partly because he wanted to know this town and its people as he had known New Salem, he was daily more deeply impressed by its wealth and splendor.

There was hardly a log house in the whole city. The homes

were frame structures, or built of brick, and they spoke of a solidarity that he had never known. Someday, someday—but what of now? What of the near future, even if he reckoned it in terms of two or three years?

Mary Owens had told him to get himself established, and then renew his offer. But getting "established" in a way that would satisfy the Squire's daughter—how long would it take? She was "society" in Green County, Kentucky. She lived in a great house, and wore fine clothes, and had never taken a back seat for anybody. She had told him, repeatedly, that she could stand poverty if she knew that she was loved—but what did she know of poverty? And what did she know about love? How could she tell whether affection would make up for lack of the things she was used to, for want of even necessities?

She didn't know what she was talking about. Any more than he knew when he spoke of marriage.

Again, in his loneliness in the new town, he was confronted by the actualities of marriage, and again, he was afraid.

Could he, in any decency, assume responsibility for another's happiness? He, who had never found the key to it for himself? He had had high moments, times of exaltation and soul-satisfaction when he had finished a hard job, won a difficult battle in the House, or helped a friend. But day-to-day contentment, free of doubts and fear and unfilled hunger for something better, he had never known. He wondered whether he would ever know it.

For he realized now that he would always be driven, driven by an ambition that was not capable of satiation, or even of peace. Could he lash any woman to the unbending mast of that ambition?

Mary had seemed to understand that drive, but she didn't know, any more than she knew hardship, what would be the practical effect of his ambition upon any woman who shared his life with him. She didn't know anything about the black moods that so often possessed him and his need for human comfort at those times, or the inability of any human being to break through the dark fog and comfort him.

Anyhow, he thought now, a little testily, as he walked the streets of Springfield in the evening and saw the young married couples flourishing about in carriages, the like of which he couldn't buy with a whole year's earnings, anyhow, hadn't Mary been a little too compliant, a little too eager the last time he saw her?

She hadn't given him a definite answer, but she'd seemed almost anxious — after keeping him dangling all these months! He'd be the first to admit that his prospects were better than they had been last fall, but his immediate situation, as far as marriage was concerned, was worse. For living costs in Springfield were ten times what they were in New Salem, and twice what it took to live in Vandalia. And wasn't he, himself, subsisting without expense at all, rooming with Joshua Speed—ah, there was a lad for you—educated, charming, quick to friendship! And boarding, for nothing, with the Butler family! If Mary should come to him now, he'd be hog-tied to know how to feed her!

As day followed day with no callers at the office except friends who dropped in to speculate about the new capital building—what it would look like, how much it would cost, where the money was coming from and when—or the price of hogs, Abe became more and more skeptical as to the definite time when he would be "established." That time seemed to recede, like a mirage, the closer he got to it, until it was always out of reach.

Of course, he'd given Mary his word. He'd made her an honorable proposition. He couldn't go back on that and keep on living with himself.

But if something should happen to make her decide definitely that she didn't want to marry him—if she should give him an irrevocable "No," and end the uncertainty and also the obligation . . . . .

Actually, he argued with himself, she'd be much better off if she decided against him. He'd never be able to give her any kind of comfort, and he might as well admit it. There was no sense in fooling himself or her. He'd painted pretty dreams for her, bright stories of his "prospects." But he hadn't said much about his present. He hadn't told her he was living on charity.

If he should write her now just how things were with him, she'd have no difficulty at all in deciding what she wanted.

His letter must be very carefully worded, though. She mustn't be allowed to suspect that she was being persuaded against him, that he was reluctant to keep his word. No, he must only tell her the truth and let her judge for herself. The real picture should be persuasion enough!

He was so very circumspect that it took three starts to satisfy him, but when he had finished writing he was almost pleased with himself. He wrote how lonely he had been. "I have been spoken to by but one woman since I've been here, and should not have been by her, if she could have avoided it."—That had been an amusing and embarrassing experience, in Speed's store one day, when he had been so absorbed in an argument with Joshua that he had turned quickly away from the counter, and all but collided with a pretty young customer. He had murmured a quick and confused apology, and she had answered politely. She was little and pert, and beautifully dressed, and his curiosity had been roused enough to ask Speed after she had left who she was. His friend told him she was a sister-in-law of the town's self-appointed aristocrat, Ninian Edwards, who was here from Lexington to visit Edward's wife, her sister Elizabeth. Abe had thought no more about her until this day, but, he remembered ruefully, he wasn't storying Mary any. The girl wouldn't have spoken to him if she hadn't had to!

Of course, Mrs. Butler spoke to him, but that was different. He still wasn't lying. . . . .

He wrote Mary of the gay social life in Springfield, which she could not join if she were to come here to live, and he reminded her that while she might be willing to entertain poverty, she didn't really know what it was, or what she'd be getting into. She'd better think it over maturely before she decided. Of course, he was willing to abide by her studied decision, but—emboldened now by his own eloquence—he'd advise her, for her own good, not to tackle it.

He ended the letter on a wistful note that he hoped would rouse her sympathy, and also convince her of his sincerity. "You must write me a good long letter after you get this. . . .

it would be a good deal of company to me in this 'busy wilderness.'" And, "Tell your sister I don't want to hear any more about selling out and moving. That gives me the hypo whenever I think of it."

He read the letter over before he mailed it. Yes, it was sincere. Every word of it was true. Moreover, it was fair. No woman could ask more of a man. And perhaps, at least, it would bring him a definite answer. . . . . .

Chapter Twenty Five

*O*NE SENTENCE IN ABE'S LETTER PIQUED MARY MORE THAN all the rest of the gloomy epistle. It was his admonition to write him a "good long letter," because, he had added thoughtlessly, "you have nothing else to do."

Well, she had plenty else to do. There was Betsey's enormous family and the housework to help with, there were her old friends whom she had known before they had moved here from Kentucky, life-long friends, and all the new ones she had made during her long stay in Illinois. There were letters from home, and answers to be written back to her family. She had a great deal to do besides jump to Abe Lincoln's bidding, as though his slightest whim should be a command to her!

Moreover, he'd waited long enough to write to her when he, admittedly, had nothing else to do! If he were in love with her at all, he certainly took a strange way of showing it! She seemed to be much more on his mind than on his heart—as though she were a legal problem which must be weighed judiciously, considering all the technicalities!

Yet, she knew that he was subject to moods and to melancholy. She recalled that other peculiar letter, that she had

had from him in December, when he had asked for "something to amuse" him. He had told her something of those spells of emotional depression which took hold of him at times without warning, but she hadn't much believed him. She'd thought he was only playing on her sympathy. But maybe they were real. Perhaps he did need amusing.

Just the same, she hardly knew what to write back. If, as it seemed on the face of the letter, he was trying to back out of his bargain—well, no man would ever get the chance to jilt Mary Owens!

But if his letter was prompted only by "the hypo," if he were really lonely and disappointed at the slowness of his fortunes . . . . .

She decided she had better give him the benefit of doubt. Write him an easy, friendly letter, that would commit neither of them, leave each a way out if necessary.

So she wrote him she was sorry he found Springfield such a dull place after all these weeks, and so devoid of attractive women. She wondered if he were not making mountains out of molehills, conjuring up conditions which did not exist. Perhaps the country air might do him some good. He ought to come back to New Salem for a visit while things were so slow in Springfield. Then she added the only real news, unpleasant as it was, that Bennett was still trying to sell his farm, and that he vowed and declared he was moving to Missouri as soon as he could find someone to take the place off his hands.

That was the best she could do, without either damaging her pride or taking advantage of what might be, in him, only a mood. But, as she posted the letter, she wondered whether she'd ever understand him any better than he did her. They seemed to be at cross-purposes all the time, with never any of that meeting of the minds which they had both found so stimulating in their early friendship. She also wondered, tiredly, what was to come of it. Anything, anything at all?

Chapter Twenty Six

ALL THE WAY BACK TO NEW SALEM ON HORSEBACK, ABE pondered his next move. Mary's reply to his careful letter surprised him, and left him entirely befuddled. He had thought he was using the same strategy which had been so successful in the Legislature—playing both ends against the middle—but perhaps those tactics wouldn't work with a woman. Had he been too subtle, or not subtle enough? Had he protested sincerity when any woman with a mind could figure out that he was just trying to get out of his bargain? Or had he convinced her so well of his sincerity that she thought all he wanted was reassurance that she could stand poverty with him?

He was so bewildered that he decided the only thing to do was to take her advice and visit New Salem again. This time, this time—he swore the strongest oath that anyone had ever heard him utter—by jing, he was going to have an answer, one way or the other!

But he was afraid of the answer, too. He was mortally scared that, convinced at last that he wouldn't wait any longer, she'd up and say yes.

Well, he was here, and he was in for it, win, lose or draw.

However, he lingered awhile in the village, just to put off the showdown, and to talk over again, with whomever might be around, the increasing disintegration of the town. The breakup was slow, as though the village, knowing it was doomed, stubbornly hung on to life through sheer force of will. It was having an agonizing death, painful to watch, and yet he couldn't force himself to look away until it was over, until he was sure that no remedy would help.

There was hardly anyone around to talk to, however. He found only the growing dilapidation of cabins where people used to live; the old cooper shop caving in; Doc Reginer's combined home-and-office boarded up so long that the boards were falling off; grass grown wild as hay for want of a sickle.

He rode on through town and out toward the Abells', wondering what he'd say to Mary.

The farm was still in good repair, the flower garden thriving.

And Betsey was flourishing like the green bay tree, and pregnant as usual!

"Betsey," he greeted her, "you're a fine sight for my tired old eyes! And I vow that in all Springfield there's no woman can cook like you!"

Betsey laughed. "How many women's cooking have you eaten in Springfield?" she demanded. She wanted to know, to find out whether his procrastination with Mary was due to a rival or his own poor sense—or Mary's contrariness.

"Only William Butler's wife," he admitted, and then, spying Mary among the confusion of children, he decided he'd better forget the levity, and get down to business. It was a warm day, and they all sat down out in the yard. Betsey, as usual whenever Abe arrived, sent one of the youngsters to bring Bennett in from the field.

"Springfield's a mighty fancy town," Abe told the girls while they waited for Bennett. "Folks step high and lively there. And there's a passel of lawyers even for a town that size."

Betsey wanted to be told about the stores, and the fine carriages, and the women's clothes. And the schools. Mary listened, considering; wondering how much of his talk was deliberate; trying to see his intention through the smoke screen of light talk.

"The stores are fine," Abe told Betsey, "with all make of brought-on goods. Kid gloves for the ladies, and dried fruits, and victuals we couldn't get in New Salem. And fancy prices on them," he added, stealing a glance at Mary to see how she was taking his recital. "When the Legislature gets moved, prices will likely go up, too, because of the increased demand. Living quarters will be almost impossible to get."

He switched then to Joshua Speed, his hospitality, his charm, what a fine friend he was. The girls readily accepted Abe's valuation, for wasn't Speed from Kentucky? He was home folks, and was bound to be a splendid person.

"Why don't you bring him out some time, for us to meet?" demanded Betsey. But Mary thought it would be better for her and Betsey to visit Springfield to meet Abe's friend, and see the sights.

"Springfield must be as exciting as—as Bardstown!" exclaimed Mary. "And when the Legislature moves, there'll be receptions, and parties, and good talk!"

That wasn't at all the kind of reaction Abe had planned and hoped for when he told the girls about the bright life in the city.

"We haven't had a real case yet," he put in hastily, "though Stuart's a good lawyer. He's known all around the country."

Mary started to remind him that since court wasn't in session, he could hardly expect much legal work. But she caught herself just in time, her suspicion hardening into realization. His detailing of his position was deliberate, and regardless of the reason (she'd have to have time to think that out) she could think of no counter at all.

"You're just in time for the outing tomorrow," she told him. "There's a crowd of us going to ride over to Uncle Billy Greene's farm, on horseback. It will be an all-day affair and we'll pack a lunch. Can you stop over for that?"

Abe reckoned he could, tired of the battle of wits. It would be something to do, and a respite from talk. It would give him a breathing spell, and time to plan what to do and say next.

Mary knew quite well how attractive she was in her riding habit. The skirt was of brown alpaca, with a bright-colored jacket, and it had been made by a tailor at home who knew how to fashion such things. She pinned her hat on at an angle, and was aware that she sat a side-saddle well. Bennett had loaned her one of his best horses, and the saddle was good leather, with a red carpet seat. The bridle jingled with

German silver, and Mary Owens made a handsome figure indeed.

She was so very handsome that her escort appeared more grotesque than ever. He'd had to wear his long-tailed lawyer coat, having no other with him, and his stovepipe hat. His stirrups, designed for a man of ordinary height, brought his knees alarmingly close to his chin, and he looked more like a scarecrow than anything human, when the two started out toward the village to join their party.

They were both determined to forget—or put off—their differences for the day and to have a good time.

Mary wanted to show Abe and the others what a good horsewoman she was, and as the party left New Salem, she urged her horse to a brisk gallop, so that she and Abe soon left the rest far behind.

The air was good, the horses in fine fettle, and Mary's spirits rose as they raced along, first one ahead, then the other. Abe reached the ford of the stream first, and looking ahead, Mary saw that some of the others had also got there by taking a cross-cut. The earlier arrivals were crossing the stream by the time Mary approached, and she noticed with satisfaction that the men were helping their ladies across with a deference and solicitation that she would not have expected of them. They were nice young men, in spite of their pioneer upbringing. Perhaps it wouldn't be bad to live the rest of her life among these people, after all.

Then she saw, amazedly, Abe Lincoln splashing through the water across the ford, without even a backward glance at her. He was having a great time trying to keep his long legs out of the water, and to guide the horse with one hand while he clung to his tall hat with the other.

He worked his horse across onto the far bank, and shouted back to the others, highly pleased with himself. Apparently, he hadn't given one thought to his companion.

Mary was furious. It wasn't as though she couldn't get across the stream by herself, although it was known to be treacherous. His flagrant discourtesy humiliated her, and when he calmly sat astride his horse and watched her negotiate the stream, as though she were another man, she was so angry that she forgot her own manners, too.

"You're a nice fellow!" she stormed when she had got safely across. "I suppose you didn't care whether my neck was broken or not!"

Abe was taken sharply aback, and was hardly less humiliated by her outburst before their friends than she was by his neglect. "Why, I thought you were plenty smart to take care of yourself," he stammered, and then added, "You're an excellent horsewoman, Mary. You did mighty well."

"That isn't the point at all!" she flared. "The point is, you embarrassed me in front of everybody! As though—as though you didn't care what happened to me!"

She was immediately sorry, for she knew that he hadn't come on this trip just to offend her. His oversight was—an oversight. He simply didn't know any better. But that knowledge was no consolation, either. The day, the ride, were spoiled for her, and no amount of rationalization could undo the damage.

The trip was spoiled for Abe, too. For, whether he wanted to marry her or not, he had no desire to hurt her. And the incident only deepened his sense of inadequacy with women, and strengthened his doubt that he could ever make any woman happy. He seemed to have a genius for doing the wrong thing as far as women were concerned. Mary would surely be better off without him.

But after that, he couldn't press her for an answer. He didn't want her to decide when she was angry. He wanted her to be sure, after calm deliberation, that she didn't want to marry him.

So he returned to Springfield to wait for a law case, with his romance unchanged and dangling like a frayed rope hanging from a rafter, waiting for one or the other to hang himself with it.

Chapter Twenty Seven

$\mathcal{B}$ACK IN SPRINGFIELD, LIFE WASN'T QUITE AS DULL AS IT had been before Abe's disastrous visit to New Salem.

While he and Stuart were finding the law business as dry as the parched Illinois prairie, banks were beginning to fail throughout the whole west, and the repercussions were reaching the boom town. There was talk of a special meeting of the Legislature at Vandalia to suspend specie payments by the Springfield State Bank, and on the fifth of June, Governor Duncan issued a proclamation convening the lawmakers on July 10.

Abe was too disturbed over this development to think about marriage. If the rumbling panic became real, what would happen to the internal improvements voted last winter? If the Springfield Bank closed, how could they build a new state house and move the capital? If these two projects failed, what would become of the ambitious and impractical Representative who had fought so hard for them?

He knew that in the coming special session he would have to defend his stand and fight for his pet projects. The stakes were high, for he stood to lose not only the accomplishment of the improvements and the removal of the seat of government, but his own leadership of the Whig Party in the House.

Fortunately, some diversion was offered in a local squabble over a land title, which was to remain a political side issue for a year to come.

In the spring, a Mary Anderson and her son Richard had come to Springfield to get possession of and sell ten acres of land which had belonged to their deceased husband and father, Joseph Anderson. When they arrived, they had found the place in the possession of James Adams, a lawyer, who claimed that Anderson had deeded the property to him before his death.

Mrs. Anderson asked Lawyer Lincoln to help her. The ten acres weren't worth much, but when Abe looked over the records, he thought he smelled a dead rat. For one thing, the deeds on the recorder's books didn't agree with the originals which the recorder got for him from Adams. And among the original deeds, Abe and Benjamin Talbott, the recorder, found an assignment of a judgment from Anderson to Adams which was dated before the date of entry of the judgment, and which, moreover, was all in Adams' handwriting, and signed by Anderson only with his mark.

Abe was convinced that the assignment was a forgery, and Adams based his whole claim to the property on the strength of that document. So Abe persuaded Stephen Logan to join him and Stuart in a suit against Adams, and the three, with their tongues in their cheeks, vowed the land was worth two thousand dollars.

That was on June 22, and Adams promptly filed something that he claimed was the original assignment, to which Anderson's name was signed in full.

The whole thing outraged Abe's sense of justice. He was sure that Adams had got hold of the widow's mite of land by fraud, and he aimed to straighten it out.

But there was a political angle to the case which delighted Abe, and gave him just the kind of opportunity he needed for sharpening up his wits against the coming special session of the Legislature. For Adams was running on the Democratic ticket for the office of probate judge, against Dr. A. G. Henry, the Whig candidate.

The Democrats were too strong for the comfort of the Whigs, and moreover, Adams was personally popular. He was one of the oldest settlers in Springfield, a frontier lawyer, and he had a host of friends.

Abe discovered, in rooting around for evidence in the Anderson matter, that there was some question in the town where he lived as to how Adams had obtained the property. It had belonged to a man named Sampson, and Adams' title rested on a document about which there was still some doubt.

That was meat for Abe, and he promptly sent in to the *Sangamo Journal* a letter signed "Sampson's Ghost," demanding that Adams just tell the people how he got the land that he was living on. It was a side issue which would accomplish just as much as if Adams were accused in the paper of getting the Anderson property by fraud—and would deflect suspicion from Abe Lincoln as the writer of the letter, for it was on the Anderson deal that Abe was of record.

"Sampson's Ghost" got Adams' dander up—he must have a guilty conscience there too, thought Abe—and the show was on. Adams replied in the Democratic paper, and the see-sawing kept up all summer. (In spite of all this, Adams won his election, but the fracas eased the tension during the hot, inactive months.)

Daniel Webster's visit to Springfield was a more momentous event which deflected Abe's thoughts away from his frustrated love affair. Captain Merryman and a mounted company rode out miles from town on the Jacksonville road to meet the great orator, and Whigs gathered from all over the county to hear him. A barbecue was held in a grove near Springfield—there wasn't a building in town big enough to hold the crowd!—and Webster talked for over an hour. "Never will I support a Treasury Bank!" thundered the great New Englander. "To that experiment is due the present distress of the country! .... Stand by the Constitution!"

Abe listened, marveling, and knew that he was hearing a man of larger caliber than he had ever heard before. And his dreams grew taller, listening. . . . .

Along in July, the Long Nine themselves were toasted in a banquet at the Rural Hotel, along with Archibald Williams and Orville Browning and McClernand, in a celebration for several members of the Legislature who were passing through town. And if Browning didn't get up, before the seventy guests, and declare that the passage of the Internal Improvements and Seat of Government Bills were entirely the work of the Sangamon Delegation! They drank toasts to everybody and everything in Illinois, and at last Abe himself got up enough gumption to rise and offer a toast: "To all our friends—they are too numerous to be now named individually, while there is no one of them who is not too dear to be forgotten or neglected!"

Abe was riding high, and the summer wasn't wasted, after all.

Chapter Twenty Eight

IT WASN'T UNTIL THE MIDDLE OF AUGUST THAT ABE GOT around to reconsideration of Mary Owens. By that time, it took quite a mental leap to get back into the state of mind in which he'd left his lagging affair.

He had come out of his morbid fears of the whole situation, however, and all he wanted now was a definite answer. He didn't care whether he married the woman or not. If he should, he could contemplate matrimony without unholy fright or great elation. If he shouldn't marry her, he wouldn't be much cast down. All he wanted was to find out whether he was going to or not.

So he rode out to New Salem again, confident that at last he could command the situation. He was the Whig leader in the House, and he'd stand for no more evasions!

This visit offered him more than a showdown with Mary. He was still trailing clouds of the glory of that Long Nine banquet, and he wanted to tell Bennett about it. And he was anxious to learn his friend's plans, though he had given up hoping that Bennett would not go away. There was no reason for anyone to linger on at New Salem.

Abe found the Abells in the midst of a birthday celebration. Betsey was thirty-three years old that 16th day of August, 1837. And she was just up and around after her last baby, another boy. So there were two reasons for celebration.

"We're runnin' out of names for the young'uns, Abe," Betsey greeted him, "This one we just called William, for no reason except it's a good name."

"It's a fine name," responded Abe, looking around for Mary, determined to get his business with her finished, and then enjoy himself afterwards.

But Bennett cornered him immediately.

"What they goin' to do about the road between here and Petersburg?" he demanded.

Abe had to tell him that the proposed road was not to go from New Salem to Petersburg, but from Beardstown to Petersburg, nowhere near New Salem, but that the bill was being held over for a third reading, and hadn't been voted on.

"If that road was to go from New Salem—" speculated Bennett. But it would take more than a road to save New Salem, and they both knew it. Bennett's next remark admitted that knowledge.

"Betsey's brother out in Missouri says there's nothin' like the rich bottom land along the big river. He's been there nigh onto ten years, and he wouldn't have stayed if it hadn't been good. Land is cheap out there, too, and you can buy a farm sight unseen, without havin' two-thirds of it turn out to be a hill. And the Mississipp' is deep enough to float a battleship."

That old rankling resentment against the Sangamon that had never fulfilled its promise! Abe nodded in sympathy, only half-listening, trying to keep his eye on Mary, who seemed to be uncommonly busy all of a sudden, in and out of the house, trying to help Betsey, fussing over the children. "And now with the boys nigh grown, I could handle a good-sized farm. . . . ." It appeared Bennett was set to talk all day.

Mary was looking wonderfully attractive in a summery flowered challis dress, with her curls all beautifully in place, and her face flushed with the excitement of Betsey's birthday celebration.

Watching her, and unable to get a word in edgewise with her, Abe began to hope against what he considered his better judgment, that she'd decide to marry him after all! Anyhow, she was in a fine good humor today, and if Bennett ever got through talking Missouri. . . . .

But when Bennett got through talking Missouri, with Abe nodding confirmation to he didn't know what wild speculation, the nearest neighbors came in with a "surprise" cake for the party, and the rest of the afternoon was spent eating, toasting Betsey, and picking the bones of New Salem. These folks were his own, they had helped to make him what he was, and Abe couldn't break away from them when they were so eager to hear stories of his success, not even to propose again to Mary Owens.

Moreover, as the afternoon wore on, he became aware that she was deliberately avoiding him. She was cordial, and as interested in his exploits as ever, but she kept the room between them, and was careful to stay close to the other women, so that he couldn't approach her. Betsey caught his eye now and then, and tried to flash him encouragement, for her intuition told her that this visit of Abe's had not been prompted by mere social yearnings. But there was nothing Betsey could do about the situation, either. She couldn't send her other guests home, and even if she had, she couldn't control her sister.

So, as the shadows began to grow tall, and still he hadn't been able to get a word alone with Mary, Abe decided he would have to start the twenty-mile horseback ride back to Springfield, and count this visit lost, too.

An unusual fatigue settled on him as he turned the horse toward New Salem. For he could not deny the look in Bennett Abell's eyes when he told his friend goodbye. Abe had seen that look in the faces of too many pioneers not to know what it meant—that soon Bennett would be off again, in search of the wonderstone, and that there would be few, if any, more gatherings in comradeship at the Abell farm north of New Salem. That part of Abe's life would soon be gone, forever. . . . .

And, watching his progress into the dusk, Mary Owens was saddened too. For she knew what her answer to him must be. She had known for quite a while now.

Chapter Twenty Nine

$\mathcal{P}$ERHAPS IT WAS ONLY HIS UNHAPPINESS OVER BENNETT'S possible removal from New Salem, perhaps it was the uncertainty of his own financial condition, maybe it was reaction from the strain of the long summer and the problems that he knew he would have to tackle in the next session of the Legislature. But Abe knew, as he journeyed slowly back toward Springfield, that his patience with Mary Owens was exhausted. He had waited long enough. He had been fair enough. He'd given her every consideration possible. She'd asked for time, and he'd given her time. Time enough to win a war or plot a revolution. Time enough to fall into love or out of love. What was love, anyhow? Surely, it was more than the admiration he felt for Mary when she was in her good moods. Surely, it was more than the excitement that had shaken him that day last fall in the woods. He'd known that excitement before, and hadn't connected it mentally with any idea of marriage. He wasn't even sure that that wonder and amazement should be expected in marriage. Were desire and respect reconcilable with a woman like Mary?

He didn't know. One thing he did know. And that was that the wonder and the desire had been lost in that uncertain moment in the woods, and he'd never recaptured them again with Mary. What to blame for that—his clumsiness, her reluctance, or only circumstances—he didn't know. Maybe they'd talked too much. If they'd ever had a chance for love together, they'd talked it away, killed it with too many words, too much thinking, weighing of pros and cons, like judges sitting in chancery.

However, mulling over the whole thing as he jogged along in the moonlight, trying to think it out, he came back again to the same intolerable situation: he had asked Mary Owens to marry him, and she wouldn't give him an answer.

He wanted to continue to be fair with her, but now, after all these months, he was certainly entitled to ordinary courtesy from her, and it was her duty to make the thing definite and clear cut, and final.

By the time he reached Springfield, the old familiar melancholy possessed him so completely that he knew he would have no peace until he did something to force the situation. His visit had failed. The only course left to him was to write to her and demand an answer.

It was late, and Speed was in bed when he arrived, but Abe lit a candle, and, sitting with his back toward the bed to shield his friend against the light, he tackled the job as painstakingly as though he were pleading in court. In fact, reading it over as he wrote, he feared the letter would appear just about as inspired as a court pleading. But the time had gone beyond need or possibility of pretty phrases. This letter was simply a statement of facts.

As a statement of facts, there was little he could say that could be pleasing to her. So he told her, "Perhaps any other man would know enough without further information; but I consider it *my* peculiar right to plead ignorance, and your bounden duty to allow the plea."

Then, because he must be fair, he urged her, "If you feel yourself in any degree bound to me, I am now willing to release you, provided you wish it; while, on the other hand, I am willing, and even anxious, to bind you faster, if I can be convinced that it will . . . . add to your happiness." And, after some hesitation, he added, for emphasis, "I think I can not be misunderstood; to make myself understood is the only object of this letter."

But he wanted to be kind. So he suggested that if she should not answer his letter at all, he would take that as her dismissal of him. At least, he could make a refusal easy for her. He even hoped that, since refusal by silence would be the easiest way out for her, she would take that way.

Now, at last, the die was cast. He knew that this time, Mary could not evade. He had forced the issue, and she'd have to do something about it.

He tumbled into bed beside Joshua, exhausted, but calm, almost at peace. In that security, he slept.

Chapter Thirty

$\mathcal{M}$ ARY TOOK ABE'S LETTER OUT TO THE BACK YARD TO READ, and sat down under a tree with it. Betsey was entirely too curious. She had sensed climax in the air the other day when Abe was here, and she hadn't stopped talking since, trying to convince Mary that she should marry Abe at once, or at least promise, because he had reached such a point in his career that if Mary didn't grab him now, he might get away forever!

Mary knew that just as well as Betsey did, and she didn't need any advice. She could make her own decisions. In fact, , she had already made this one.

Looking back now over their acquaintanceship, Mary wondered that she had ever been in any doubt. Perhaps she had been impressed by Betsey's praise of the man and her glowing predictions of his success. Mary did not doubt for a moment that he would know the success that Betsey hoped for him. She had seen in him, herself, the power and the drive, and the ability to climb any height that he might choose, to reach his goal. Nothing could stop him.

She had thought, for a little while, that perhaps the right woman could help him get there a little faster than he could climb alone. A woman of education, and background, and social experience.

She still believed it. But what would his wife have in return?

She would share his success. Whatever glory might come to him, his wife would be at his side, knowing that she had had her part in his accomplishment.

She would be at his side, but he would never be at her side.

Abe Lincoln's wife would never know a lover, or a husband, or even a companion. She would know his ambition. She would eat it, sleep with it, live it, and her life would be bent to its shape. She would taste his success, or his heartache, his struggle, his doubt, his fear. He would never know hers, because he would never be able to understand it.

Mary Owens didn't want fame, or glory, or acclaim, or even modest political limelight. She wanted happiness.

She didn't want money, or the things money could buy, of themselves. Never having known poverty, she could still chance it with a man who could give her what she needed more than comfort—love, tenderness, and consideration. She had comfort. It was love she was hungry for.

Because she was a woman, she knew that the ingredients of happiness are the little things, the minutiae of inconsequentials that make up the day and the bulk of human living. Would broken shoes matter if a man told her he loved her? Would dry bread be hard to eat if a kiss went with it? Well, maybe it would be, but it would be easier with a kiss than without.

Abe Lincoln would never be able to make any woman happy, because he had no purchase upon happiness himself.

Almost no capacity for it. Elation, yes. The great excitement that comes from struggle, and accomplishment, the knowledge of a hard battle won. But that wasn't happiness. That wasn't the warp and woof of contentment.

His lack, she was convinced now, was more than want of training, of social experience. It was a fundamental, inborn want of sensitivity to the nuances of living. What a musician would call an ear for music. What an artist would term an eye for color. What a woman would call . . . .

It wasn't the fact that he had never been taught to carry a woman's burdens up a hill or to help her across a stream. It was the fact that he had no capacity for learning that kind of consideration. Innate kindness and goodness he possessed in plenty, but without the ability to translate them into action or words.

Against his very real ability, Mary weighed his shortcomings, and knew her answer to the letter before she opened the envelope. She was only wondering how she could write him without hurting him too deeply, without telling him just why she couldn't marry him.

As she read his laboriously phrased evasions, she discovered another quality in his strangely mixed personality that would keep any woman from being happy with him— vacillation. In his personal life, he would never know quite what he wanted, and he'd look before and after, weighing the ifs against the might-be's, always wondering, never sure. Mary Owens wanted a husband who, though he might never be great, would be sure, and who would be a staff for her to lean on in her moments of weakness.

Then, reading the letter again, she smiled ruefully at the ironical kindness of it. In his last epistle—for this would be the last—he had shown her more consideration than at any time in their acquaintance. For he had absolved her of any need to answer. He wrote that if she did not write him at all, he would understand.

As she tucked the letter away, she felt only relief that this strange romance was over. Now she was free of any obligation to Abe Lincoln, free of her own indecision. Now— why, now, she could go home!

Chapter Thirty One

As day followed long August day after Abe had returned to Springfield, with no letter from Mary, he knew at last that there would be none, that she had taken seriously his admonition that she need not answer unless she cared to go on with him.

He wished now that he had demanded a reply, that he had not let her off so easily, for the interval of time which he had to allow before he could be sure of her unworded refusal was as difficult to get through as all the other procrastination had been.

The waiting was even harder because activity in Springfield seemed to have come to an absolute halt. With the exception of Adams' reply, in the *Illinois Republican,* to the handbill Abe had circulated about and against him, time itself stood still for two weeks, and there was nothing to do but talk to Speed in the store, or wander about the streets of the town, and dream of the new capital, monument to Illinois of his handiwork—and wonder where the money was to come from to build it.

And to search his own heart and try to discover how he really felt about Mary Owens.

It wasn't Mary he regretted. He had hoped for her refusal, and, as her silence lengthened, he reckoned he had it.

No, it was his doubt of himself that tormented him in the long August days and breathless nights, when his general inactivity forced him to worry at the thing, trying to figure it out.

For he knew that if he had cared enough for Mary, if he had even wanted her enough, he would never have been torn by doubt. He would never have considered the handicaps of marriage; he would have disregarded them as blithely as any other young man in love, and would have thought only of the joy that she could give him, she, and no other woman on earth. And he would have battered down her resistance, would have convinced her irrevocably that her only happiness was in his hands.

He had wanted to love her. There had been several interludes when he had thought that he did. She had everything that even an ambitious man could want in a wife—beauty, brains, education, knowledge of the ways of society that could be learned only through gracious living. She had poise, charm, and she was essentially kind.

Why, then, hadn't he loved her enough? Enough to still his doubt and hers? Enough to lose himself in the happiness within his reach?

As he mulled it over and over during the hot, sleepless nights when even "Sampson's Ghost" was too lethargic to distract him from his brooding, a greater doubt and fear crept into his heart to stay, and he could not eradicate it. A fear that he would never be satisfied with the thing at hand, the prize within his reach—whether it be a woman or a law case or a political office; that always, he would be straining on, to the next hill, the next valley, the farther mountain, lashed and driven by a mistress whom he would never conquer—ambition. Ambition was the only emotion he had ever known intimately, the only urge that could possess all of him; the only passion that could consume him.

He could look ahead now, where before he had seen as in a mirror, darkly, and his way was clear. He knew where he was going now. It was a straight road that stretched ahead of him, but a narrow one, with room for only one to walk. He would go alone. Though he knew that he would have friends and many moments of happiness; though he might and probably would marry some day (some woman would get him sure, some woman who wanted him more than Mary Owens had); still, he would go alone, a man turned into himself, guided only by his own peculiar beacon, known by no man, owned by no woman. . . . .

Speed, lying beside him in the double bed, slept lightly, peacefully. Not a stirring of air came in through the window off the breathless prairie, but Abe Lincoln felt a chill ripple through him, and the aspen tree outside shivered a hushed sigh, though there was no wind blowing. . . . .

Epilogue

S PRING IN MISSOURI WAS LIKE IT HAD BEEN IN KENTUCKY, early and gentle and lazy, drifting over the land like a dream, with a sweetness as poignant as youth, stirring memories that had long been blanketed under the winter snow.

But it wasn't only the May breeze, heavy with lilac fragrance, that turned Mary Owens Vineyard's thoughts back over the years, back to New Salem and a different Spring.

There was that letter of William Herndon's that must be answered.

It didn't seem decent to pry into a woman's personal affairs as this man was trying to do, or into the private life of a man like Abraham Lincoln. But, Abe's one-time law partner wrote her, he had been trying, in the year since the President's death, to gather together all available material about his old friend for a personalized biography. He'd been talking with and writing to everyone who had ever known Abe, and someone who remembered New Salem had recalled Mary Owens, and the days when he'd courted her.

This book that Herndon was planning was one, he urged, that should be written, for there had been so much misunderstanding, so much recrimination and idolization of the man whom both Herndon and Mary had known so well.

Mr. Herndon wanted to write a true account of Abe Lincoln, to draw a picture of the great man, as a man. And there was no one in the country better able to write truthfully of that enigmatic character than William Herndon, who had worked with him, practiced law with him, lived with him.'

Abe Lincoln had gone farther than even she or Betsey had been able to predict. They had both recognized the power in him, the selflessness that had made him at once the humblest and most conceited man they had ever known, the compassion which was almost superhuman in its proportions.

Only Mary had seen the predictable results of that quality, and even she had not been able to put it precisely into words —she had sensed it only: the quality that made him belong so much to the people, to all humanity, that he could not be compassed, could not belong to any one person—not even to himself.

But neither Mary nor her sister had been surprised when he was elected President, to steer the country through the most cruel and senseless war in history.

What had surprised Mary was his marriage to the daughter of one of the proudest families in Kentucky. She guessed, shrewdly, that Mary Todd had married him, had wanted him so much, that by the sheer force of her will she had conquered his vacillation. Mary Todd had seen in him the same capacity for greatness that Mary Owens had recognized. But Mary Todd had seen nothing else. She had been blind to the other facets of his character, to those woeful lacks that would preclude any possibility of happiness for the woman who married him. Mary Vineyard didn't need the rumors of his widow's insanity to know that the First Lady had never known happiness with Abe. It wasn't only his horrible murder that had contributed to that mental derangement. It was the piling up, year after year, into that awful climax, of disappointment and loneliness and hurt.

For Mary Vineyard knew that Mary Lincoln, in her happiness, in her pain, in her most intimate moments with her husband, had always been alone.

Mary Owens had been happy. Quietly, normally, glowingly happy.

She'd gone back home in the spring of '38, reconciled to a life of spinsterhood in her father's household, convinced that the only children she'd ever hold in her arms would be the babies of her sisters and brothers, sure that she would never know any personal joy, except the comfort of service to others.

And then, three years later, when she was no longer young, she'd married Jesse Vineyard and moved to Missouri. And she had found fulfilment in the deep, glowing fires of mature love, all the better because she'd waited so long. She was past thirty when she married.

Even so, she had been blessed five times with motherhood, and each year had enriched the soil to which she had transplanted herself, and she had known a peace and contentment, in obscurity, which Mary Lincoln, the First Lady of the Land, had never tasted.

She wasn't sorry. She had never been sorry that she hadn't hitched her wagon to that dazzling, careening star which had beckoned Abe Lincoln on and on, and up and up, until he had died at an assassin's hand because he was loved so much and hated so much.

She could have had him. She could have gone with him, and stood beside him on the high mountain, close to that blazing star. She had chosen, instead, with her eyes open, oblivion, contentment, and a woman's kind of happiness.

But she couldn't write William Herndon that. It was too personal. Anyhow, no man would ever understand. Particularly a man who had been Abe Lincoln's close and dear friend.

All Mr. Herndon wanted was facts, the events of her friendship with Lincoln, the details that could be set down in history for the prying eyes of posterity.

A formal, courteous letter, telling Lincoln's biographer what must be told, all that needed to be told, of her acquaintance with Abe back in New Salem, was all that was required.

She would answer his questions—some of them—but she would preserve her thoughts, her memories, her dignity as a woman. Give him only what history had a right to relate.

She found her paper and pen and sat down to compose the letter. It would be difficult to write, not an easy thing to do, even for a woman of her poise and command.

She stared at the blank page for a while, trying to formulate her phrases mentally. Then, with a smile half-mischievous, half-proud, that revealed the consciousness of quality that had always been a part of Nathaniel Owens' daughter, she started writing.

"Really, you catechize me in true lawyer style; but I feel you will have the goodness to excuse me if I decline answering all your questions . . . . being well assured that few women would have ceded as much as I have under all the circumstances. . . . ."

Appendix

MARY OWENS

Appendix

by
R. Gerald McMurtry

My INTEREST IN MARY OWENS GOES BACK TO SEVERAL YEARS ago, when I tramped through Green County, Kentucky, as rodman in a surveying party which was marking the first important highway to be constructed in that part of the state. While mapping the road, taking cross-sections, making topographical readings, and plotting drainage areas, I chanced to walk over a considerable portion of Nathaniel Owens' plantation on Little Brush Creek. The Georgian mansion where Mary was born still stood, in a fair state of repair.

Having then only a vague knowledge of the Lincoln-Owens love affair, I became interested in the history of this pioneer family and the lineage of the obscure woman who for a few months held Lincoln's heart and hand at her disposal.

After becoming acquainted with all the available facts and local legends concerning the proud planter and his talented daughter, I made a cursory survey of Lincoln's many courtships and read several volumes on the women he loved, only to discover eventually that many writers of the old school of biography sincerely believed that the sixteenth president was a man distracted over his unrequited love for Ann Rutledge. After considerable investigation, particularly of the later studies and discoveries, I reached the conclusion that the accounts of his romance with the New Salem lass, which portray a picturesque and romantic idyll, are unfortunately, more suppositional than factual.

Because of the romantic bent of human minds, we have devoted many columns of print to the pathetic story of Lincoln's love for Ann Rutledge, of which we know almost nothing, and seldom give more than passing mention to his affair with Mary Owens, of which there is an abundance of evidence. All because a rural maiden in pastoral New Salem —and a tragic love affair—arouse more sympathy than the almost over-educated Mary Owens or the aristocratic and spirited Mary Todd.

Within the last few years I decided to take up again the study of the interesting woman who could have had Abraham Lincoln, and turned him down, to pry into her early childhood in Kentucky, to discover how she obtained her education, to find all the facts of her romance with Lincoln, and then to learn something of her married life in Missouri.

In the compiling of this data I have had no ulterior motive in attempting to deflate the Ann Rutledge tradition, to minimize Mary Todd's influence on Lincoln, or to elevate Mary Owens out of her proper position. Yet too long have sentimentalists relegated Mary Owens to oblivion. Too often have they referred to her as merely "fashionable, educated, and born of wealth," with little or no comment on her cultural background, her character, her gay spirit, and her pleasing personality. Only brief mention has been made of her family, relatives, friends, and her high position in the society of her own Kentucky community. Some historians have contemptuously referred to her as a country girl who was attractive to Lincoln, mostly because she caught him on the rebound after Ann Rutledge's death.

A complete account of the Lincoln-Owens romance, with all the significant letters and documents pertaining to the affair, along with biographical data on Mary Owens, has not yet been collected in book form. However, the task of correlating the voluminous amount of fact and tradition regarding the courtship has not been an easy one, for while there has been ample documentary material to work with— such as plot, setting, and characterization—these facts in many cases have been unrelated and disconnected. Only the novelist using "poetic license" can weave the known events of the romance into a connected sequence of happenings, while the biographical data should be treated as an appendix. The real value of this study is that both the casual reader and the exacting student can more fully analyze and understand Lincoln during that important period of his life when he was groping about, trying to find himself. We hope that this study will also give a new portrait of a woman who had all the qualities of a Todd, who saw in him just as much as Mary Todd saw, but who voluntarily declined the road to honor and glory because he was "deficient in those little links which make up the chain of a woman's happiness."

The literature has not entirely overlooked the Lincoln-Owens romance. She has been referred to as "The Third Woman in Lincoln's Life" by Ida M. Tarbell in *The Delin-*

eator, February, 1934, while William E. Barton has devoted several paragraphs to Miss Owens in his magazine article, "Two Women Lincoln Loved," *Ladies Home Journal*, October, 1927. The affair received considerable treatment by Carl Sandburg in his inimitable style under the title "The Unfathomed Lincoln," *Pictorial Review*, beginning with the October, 1925, issue and ending with the March, 1926, number. Dr. Barton, in the *Dearborn Independent* for November 13, 1926, in an article "Verses That Lincoln Wrote," made an interesting comment concerning the courtship: "He [Lincoln] had no facility of expression in matters of love. His love letters to Mary Owens are a sad example of a courtship wholly ineffective because utterly done in prose." *Bulletin No. 25 of the Abraham Lincoln Association*, December, 1931, devotes seven pages to a phase of the story, while one of the most interesting studies is an essay entitled "Abraham Lincoln In His Relations To Women," by Julien Gordon, *Cosmopolitan*, December, 1894. This latter article, however, does not deal with any particular Lincoln courtship, but gives a more general treatment to the whole scope of Lincoln's love life.

A very satisfactory newspaper account of the romance was written by A. B. McDonald, revealing Lincoln as a hesitant suitor, which appeared in *The Kansas City Star*, December 30, 1928. In addition to articles appearing in periodicals and newspapers, brief sketches of the courtship have been recorded by scores of biographers and pamphleteers. Their story in most cases is essentially the same, a notable exception being the readable account by Barton in his popular book, *The Women Lincoln Loved* (Bobbs-Merrill Company, 1927, pps. 187-209). Also worthy of mention is the twelve-page pamphlet *Abraham Lincoln and Mary Owens,* which was published in 1922 by H. E. Barker. Jacob Louis Hasbrouck of the *Bloomington Pantagraph,* has facetiously referred to the courtship in a section of his pamphlet *Lincoln in Some of His Unheroic Hours,* 1938, with the statement that "He [Lincoln] did not take her [Mary Owens] to the movies, nor for automobile rides. . . . . Mary Owens was a big fat girl—and perhaps that explains why, unlike Ann Rutledge, she has never had any streamlined trains named for her." In the same humorous vein, the *Chicago Tribune* of December 12, 1941, sums up Lincoln's love affairs under the heading, "If This Be Treason, Make the Most of It," with the comment that, "No doubt his 'courting,' in most cases, consisted of occasional remarks such as, 'Howdy, Sis, how's your paw?'"

Some writers have considered the Lincoln-Owens courtship as a very serious and sacred affair. Henry James made the following comment upon hearing of the discovery and publication of some of Lincoln's letters to Mary Owens: "Somebody has been digging into Lincoln's correspondence so as to tell the tale of the great man's love affairs. I think such meddling is more than disrespectful, and that it is insolent and useless. If a man is entitled to any privacy whatever it certainly relates to matters so personal as his letters to a woman with whom he is in love. Even after he is dead, no alien hand has any decent right to be pawing over such missives."

As to the importance of the courtship and this Kentucky girl's influence on the life of the sixteenth president, Dr. Louis A. Warren, Director of the Lincoln National Life

Foundation, Fort Wayne, Indiana, recorded in a letter dated August 13, 1940, the following opinion: "I am very sure that Mary Owens played a greater part in Lincoln's life than Ann Rutledge."

In my compiling of this historical material, credit must be given to William H. Herndon for the discovery of the essential facts pertaining to the Lincoln-Owens courtship, which he described as "an affair of the heart which culminated in a sequel as amusing as the one with Ann Rutledge was sad." Herndon was able to do an excellent job of original research on the affair, and he related that he "experienced much difficulty in obtaining the particulars of this courtship." The Herndon-Weik story of the romance appeared in Vol. I, under chapter VII, pps. 143-61, of their work, *Herndon's Lincoln, The True Story of a Great Life,* (Belford Clarke and Company, 1889). However, Ward H. Lamon in his book, *The Life of Abraham Lincoln,* (James R. Osgood and Company, 1872, under chapter IX, pps. 172–193), was the first to publish the results of Herndon's researches on this subject, which were supplemented with additional documentary material.

Herndon, himself a native (born 1818) of Green County, Kentucky, while compiling data for a Lincoln biography, heard of the courtship and immediately started an historical investigation. He knew the Owens family by reputation, and accordingly he wrote to Mary Owens Vineyard (she had married Jesse Vineyard March 27, 1841) for a confirmation of the rumors of her courtship with Lincoln. At first she refused to answer his letters, but he was persistent, and after repeated solicitations, he persuaded her to reveal the facts and to lend him Lincoln's letters for a short while until he could make copies of them. She pledged Herndon to secrecy, hoping that her name as well as her place of residence might not be revealed. Her first letter, written from Weston, Missouri, reads as follows:

May 1, 1866

Mr. W. H. Herndon,

Dear Sir,—After quite a struggle with my feelings, I have at last decided to send you the letters in my possession written by Mr. Lincoln, believing, as I do, that you are a gentleman of honor, and will faithfully abide by all you have said.

My associations with your lamented friend were in Menard County, whilst visiting a sister, who then resided near Petersburg. I have learned that my maiden name is now in your possession; and you have ere this, no doubt, been informed that I am a native Kentuckian.

As regards Miss Rutledge, I cannot tell you any thing, she having *died* previous to my acquaintance with Mr. Lincoln; and I do not now recollect of ever hearing him mention her name. Please return the letters at your earliest convenience.

Very respectfully yours,
Mary S. ——

However, much to Herndon's disappointment, Lincoln's letters to Mary Owens did not reveal enough details of the courtship. Inquiring historian that he was, he next prepared a questionnaire for Mrs. Vineyard to answer about the entire romance from beginning to end. To Mary this was rather a delicate matter, and she was not pleased with Herndon's pointed questions. Accordingly, in a few days Lincoln's Boswell received the following letter:

WESTON, MISSOURI
May 22, 1866

MR. W. H. HERNDON,

My dear Sir,—Really you catechise me in true lawyer style; but I feel you will have the goodness to excuse me if I decline answering all your questions in detail, being well assured that few women would have ceded as much as I have under all the circumstances.

You say you have heard why our acquaintance terminated as it did. I, too, have heard the same bit of gossip; but I never used the remark which Madam Rumor says I did to Mr. Lincoln. I think I did on one occasion say to my sister, who was very anxious for us to be married, that I thought Mr. Lincoln was deficient in those little links which make up the chain of woman's happiness,—at least, it was so in my case. Not that I believed it proceeded from a lack of goodness of heart; but his training had been different from mine; hence there was not that congeniality which would otherwise have existed.

From his own showing, you perceive that his heart and hand were at my disposal; and I suppose that my feelings were not sufficiently enlisted to have the matter consummated. About the beginning of the year 1838 I left Illinois, at which time our acquaintance and correspondence ceased without ever again being renewed.

My father, who resided in Green County, Kentucky, was a gentleman of considerable means; and I am persuaded that few persons placed a higher estimate on education than he did.

Respectfully yours,
MARY S. ——

Mary's second letter to Herndon gave him one important sentence about which he later wrote to Jesse W. Weik. He said: "There is one sentence in her second letter to me dated the 22nd. May, 1866, which I shall copy—and underscore—have italicised: it is this—'I think I did on one occasion say to my sister who was very anxious for us to be married, that *I thought Mr. Lincoln was deficient in those little links which make up the chain of woman's happiness.*'" Herndon continued: "I wish that the latter part of this sentence would be kept in mind—constantly in the mind of the reader, for out of this nature of Lincoln grows—springs a sad tale."

Herndon, after receiving two letters from Mrs. Vineyard, decided another might be forthcoming if he should write her, using diplomacy and tact. He had heard a rumor about a quarrel between Miss Owens and Lincoln because of his failure to assist Mrs. Green in carrying her child up a hill. Using this as an excuse to write her, Herndon was again successful. In due time he received another letter from Mrs. Vineyard:

WESTON, MISSOURI,
July 22, 1866

MR. W. H. HERNDON

Dear Sir,—I do not think that you are pertinacious in asking the question relative to old Mrs. Bowlin Greene, because I wish to set you right on that question. Your information, no doubt, came through my cousin, Mr. Gaines Greene, who visited us last winter. Whilst here, he was laughing at me about Mr. Lincoln, and among other things spoke about the circumstances in connection with Mrs. Greene and child. My impression is now that I tacitly admitted it, for it was a season of *trouble* with me, and I gave but little heed to the matter. We never had any *hard feelings* toward each other that I know of. On no occasion did I say to Mr. Lincoln that I did not believe he would make a kind husband, because he did not tender his services to Mrs. Greene in helping her carry her babe. As I said to you in a former letter, I thought him lacking in smaller attentions. One circumstance presents itself just now to my mind's eye. There was a company of us going to Uncle Billy Greene's. Mr. Lincoln was riding with me; and we had a very bad branch to cross. The other gentlemen were very officious in seeing that their partners got over safely. We were behind, he riding in, never looking back to see how I got along. When I rode up beside him, I remarked, "You are a nice fellow! I suppose you did not care whether my neck was broken or not." He laughingly replied (I suppose by way of compliment) that he knew I was plenty smart to take care of myself.

In many things he was sensitive, almost to a fault. He told me of an incident: that he was crossing a prairie one day, and saw before him "a hog mired down," to use his own language. He was rather "fixed up;" and he resolved that he would pass on without looking towards the shoat. After he had gone by, he said the feeling was irresistible; and he had to look back, and the poor thing seemed to say wistfully, "There, now, my last hope is gone;" that he deliberately got down, and relieved it from its difficulty.

In many things we were congenial spirits. In politics we saw eye to eye, though since then we differed as widely as the South is from the North. But methinks I hear you say, "Save me from a political woman!" So say I.

The last message I ever received from him was about a year after we parted in Illinois. Mrs. Able visited Kentucky; and he said to her in Springfield, "Tell your sister that I think she was a great fool, because she did not stay here, and marry me." Characteristic of the man.

Respectfully yours,
MARY S. ——

Herndon's efforts at historical research had proved highly successful. He had copies of the three letters which Lincoln had written to Mary Owens, as well as three from Mrs. Vineyard to himself. Accordingly, with this data, in addition to other historical facts discovered elsewhere, he wrote a fifteen-page article in the form of a rough draft entitled, "Lincoln's Courtship With Miss Owens." This draft was sent to Jesse W. Weik to assist him in writing chapter VII of the Herndon-Weik biography. A photostat of the original manuscript is to be found in the files of the University of Illinois Library, a typewritten copy of which was furnished for this study by Miss Helen McIntyre. The Herndon article is of such great importance that the major portion of it has been incorporated in this Appendix.

Herndon's description of Mary Owens is quite interesting. He said that "Lincoln was evidently impressed with this maiden's looks. Probably it was the grace of her movements and the rather [?] brilliancy of her mind that charmed Lincoln. She was graceful, dignified, and rather a handsome woman. Mr. Lincoln never was spoken to by such a polished lady before. She had fine conversational powers. She was a portly woman and weighing about 170 pounds—had large blue eyes — was tall and well proportioned — was good-natured, and made all persons feel easy in her presence — was witty. However, she was free from that kind of wit that burns—bites and wilts. This lady was not beautiful by any means—was handsome because—and alone because she was a woman of commanding presence."

The Herndon biography, Vol. I, page 144, contains the following additional description of Mary Owens: "According to a description furnished me by herself she had 'fair skin, deep blue eyes, and dark curling hair; height five feet, five inches; weight about a hundred and fifty pounds.' She was good-looking in girlhood; by many esteemed handsome, but became fleshier as she grew older. One man [L. M. Greene] .... was impressed with her beauty .... years afterwards .... he wrote me: 'She was tall, portly, had large blue eyes and the finest trimmings I ever saw. She was jovial, social, loved wit and humor, had a liberal English education, and was considered wealthy. None of the poets or romance writers have ever given us a picture of a heroine so beautiful as a good description of Miss Owens in 1836 would be.' "

Herndon continued his dissertation, informing Weik that Miss Owens made two trips to Illinois. He related that "Miss Owens, the sister of Mrs. Able (Abell) came out to Illinois and as a matter of course stayed with Mrs. Able. This woman then was in her 28th year, but she did not visit long in Illinois; she went back to Kentucky, and Mrs. Able, her sister, soon paid her a visit in Kentucky in return. Mrs. Able soon returned to Illinois, bringing the same sister back with her. Lincoln resided in New Salem from '31 to '37, and it was during Miss Owens' first visit to Illinois that Lincoln first saw her." Evidently Herndon was confused about the dates of the visits, for he made the following statement: "This first visit of Miss Owens to Illinois may have been earlier than '34 (*4* marked over an original *6*) it may be as early as '33." Continuing the account he wrote: "Miss Owens returned to Illinois in 36-Octr. Mr. Lincoln was early impressed by this woman—was [a] very susceptible man. She returned to Kentucky in '38; and she was now in her 29th year and Lincoln in his 28th year."

To keep the record straight, it is well to state here that in 1833, eleven years after the marriage of her sister Betsey, Mary visited the Abells. The route she traveled to New Salem is unknown. Perhaps she went by way of a stagecoach over a turnpike from Bardstown, Kentucky, to Vincennes, Indiana, and from there over crude wagon trails to Sangamon County. After a four weeks' visit she returned to her home on Little Brush Creek. Mary's second visit to New Salem was made in the fall of 1836. She arrived there on November 7, the day Lincoln cast his vote for Senator Hugh L. White of Tennessee, the Whig candidate for president. This visit was terminated after an eighteen months period.

When Mary returned to Kentucky after her first trip, Herndon relates, "Mr. Lincoln declared that he would catch, tie, and marry this lady as soon as she returned from Kentucky; she did return to Illinois, but did Mr. Lincoln catch, tie, and marry her? Miss Owens was informed by her friends of Mr. Lincoln's intentions, and when she left Kentucky on her second trip she was determined to try his metal in his chase to catch, tie, and marry her."

In discussing the correspondence between Miss Owens and Lincoln, Herndon gave Weik the following information: "Mr. Lincoln moved to Springfield in the fall of '36 or in the spring of '37, leaving Miss Owens at Mrs. Able's. Lincoln and the lady commenced corresponding—one from Vandalia, having gone to there as [a] member of the legislature, and the other from New Salem—at least it is said so, though no letters can be found of hers." As Herndon related to Weik, no letters of Mary Owens addressed to Abraham Lincoln have ever been discovered.

In discussing Lincoln's letters to Miss Owens, Herndon was at his best in trying to read the writer's mind, thoughts, and actions. The following letter, which bears the earliest date of the three received by Mary Owens was the object of Herndon's first study.

VANDALIA, Dec. 13, 1836

MARY

I have been sick ever since my arrival here, or I should have written sooner. It is but little difference, however, as I have very little even yet to write. And more, the longer I can avoid the mortification of

207

looking in the Post Office for your letter and not finding it, the better. You see I am mad about the *old letter* yet. I dont like very well to risk you again. I'll try you once more any how.

The new State House is not yet finished, and consequently the legislature is doing little or nothing. The Governor delivered an inflamitory political Message, and it is expected there will be some sparring between the parties about it as soon as the two Houses get to business. Taylor delivered up his petitions for the *New County* to one of our members this morning. I am told he despairs of its success on account of all the members from Morgan County opposing it. There are names enough on the petition, I think, to justify the members from our county in going for it; but if the members from Morgan oppose it, which they say they will, the chance will be bad.

Our chance to take the seat of Government to Springfield is better than I expected. An Internal Improvement Convention was held here since we met, which recommended a loan of several millions of dollars on the faith of the State to construct Rail Roads. Some of the legislature are for it and some against it; which has the majority I can not tell. There is great strife and struggling for the office of U. S. Senator here at this time. It is probable we shall ease their pains in a few days. The opposition men have no candidate of their own, and consequently they smile as complacently at the angry snarls of the contending Van Buren candidates and their respective friends, as the Christian does at Satan's rage. You recollect I mentioned in the outset of this letter that I had been unwell. That is the fact, though I believe I am about well now; but that, with other things I can not account for, have conspired and have gotten my spirits so low, that I feel I would rather be any place in the world than here. I really can not endure the thought of staying here ten weeks. Write back as soon as you get this, and if possible, say something that will please me, for really I have not been pleased since I left you. This letter is so dry and stupid that I am ashamed to send it, but with my present feelings I can not do any better.

Give my best respects to Mr. and Mrs. Abell and family.

Your friend

LINCOLN

MISS MARY S. OWENS

Herndon analyzed the situation as follows: "Mr. Lincoln's first letter to Miss Owens is dated the 13th Dec. 1836; it was written from Vandalia, then the seat of government—the capital city of Illinois. Mr. Lincoln was a member of the legislature at that time and it does appear that law making was not all of his life. Part of it was given to Miss Owens. The letter—shows that Lincoln was in love—deeply in love, so much so that he felt nettled, because she had not written to him, as she had promised to do; he asks the lady to 'write back—as soon as you get this and, if possible, say something that will please me.'"

The next letter which Herndon analyzed for Weik bore a Springfield postmark:

SPRINGFIELD, May 7, 1837

FRIEND MARY,

I have commenced two letters to send you before this, both of which displeased me before I got half done, and so I tore them up. The first I thought wasn't serious enough, and the second was on the other extreme. I shall send this, turn out as it may—

This thing of living in Springfield is rather a dull business after all, at least it is so to me. I am quite as lonesome here as [I] ever was anywhere in my life. I have been spoken to by but one woman since I've been here, and should not have been by her, if she could have avoided it. I've never been to church yet, nor probably shall not be soon. I stay away because I am conscious I should not know how to behave myself—

I am often thinking about what we said of your coming to live at Springfield. I am afraid you would not be satisfied. There is a great deal of flourishing about in carriages here; which it would be your doom to see without sharing in it. You would have to be poor without the means of hiding your poverty. Do you believe you could bear that patiently? Whatever woman may cast her lot with mine, should any ever do so, it is my intention to do all in my power to make her happy and contented; and there, is nothing I can imagine, that would make me more unhappy than to fail in the effort. I know I should be much happier with you than the way I am, provided I saw no signs of discontent in you. What you have said to me may have been in jest, or I may have misunderstood it. If so, then let it be forgotten; if otherwise, I much wish you would think seriously before you decide. For my part I have already decided. What I have said I will most positively abide by, provided you wish it. My opinion is, that you had better not do it. You have not been accustomed to hardship, and it may be more severe than you now immagine.

I know you are capable of thinking correctly on any subject, and if you deliberate maturely upon this, before you decide, then I am willing to abide your decision.

You must write me a good long letter after you get this. You have nothing else to do, and though it might not seem interesting to you, after you have written it, it would be a good deal of company to me in this "busy wilderness." Tell your sister I dont want to hear any more about selling out and moving. That gives me the hypo whenever I think of it.

Yours &c—
LINCOLN

This missive was accompanied by the following comment: "The second letter of Mr. Lincoln to Miss Owens is dated May the 7th, '37; it is a curious letter and is worthy of study and is addressed to the lady from Springfield, the legislature having adjourned. I have always thought that this letter was an honest letter."

In discussing the third letter, Herndon reiterated to Weik his belief that Lincoln was honest, and he suggested a considerate judgment of the hesitant suitor.

SPRINGFIELD Aug. 16th 1837

FRIEND MARY.

You will, no doubt, think it rather strange, that I should write you a letter on the same day on which we parted; and I can only account for it by supposing, that seeing you lately makes me think of you more than usual, while at our late meeting we had but few expressions of thoughts. You must know that I cannot see you, or think of you, with entire indifference; and yet it may be, that you, are mistaken in regard to what my real feelings towards you are. If I knew you were not, I should not trouble you with this letter. Perhaps any other man would know enough without further information; but I consider it *my* peculiar right to plead ignorance, and your bounden duty to allow the plea. I want in all cases to do right; and most particularly so, in all cases with women. I want, at this particular time, more than any thing else, to do right with you, and if I *knew* it would be doing right, as I rather suspect it would, to let you alone, I would do it. And for the purpose of making the matter as plain as possible, I now say, that you can now drop the subject, dismiss your thoughts (if you ever had any) from me forever, and leave this letter unanswered, without calling forth one accusing murmur from me. And I will even go further, and say, that if it will add any thing to your comfort, or peace of mind, to do so, it is my sincere wish that you should. Do not understand by this, that I wish to cut your acquaintance. I mean no such thing. What I do wish is, that our further acquaintance shall depend upon yourself. If such further acquaintance would contribute nothing to your happiness, I am sure it would not to mine. If you feel yourself in any degree bound to me, I am now willing to release: you, provided you wish it; while, on the other hand, I am willing, and even anxious to bind you faster, if I can be convinced that it will, in any considerable degree, add to your happiness. This, indeed, is the whole question with me. Nothing would make me more miserable than to believe you miserable— nothing more happy, than to know you were so.

In what I have now said, I think I can not be misunderstood; and to make myself understood, is the only object of this letter.

If it suits you best to not answer this farewell—a long life and a merry one attend you. But if you conclude to write back, speak as plainly as I do. There can be neither harm nor danger, in saying, to me, any thing you think, just in the manner you think it.

My respects to your sister.

Your friend

LINCOLN

Herndon's analysis was as follows: "The third letter of Mr. Lincoln to Miss Owens is dated the 16th Aug. '37; it appears that Mr. Lincoln had gone down to New Salem to see her, and had returned to Springfield from which place the letter was written. Read these two letters carefully and consider that they were written by an honest man, but possibly one disposed to kick. A man that did not know Lincoln, thoroughly and well, would conclude at once that Lincoln wanted to back down, but I would ask the reader not to be too hasty in his conclusions."

In 1887 Jesse W. Weik, of Greencastle, Indiana, delved further into the question of the Lincoln-Owens courtship. He wrote Benjamin R. Vineyard, attorney-at-law in St. Joseph, Missouri, for information about his mother's romance with Lincoln, and at the same time he requested a photograph of Mary Owens to be used in the forthcoming biography. Mr. Vineyard very graciously furnished Weik with an account of the romance. (A photostat of the original document is to be found in the University of Illinois library. It was first published in its entirety in Emanuel Hertz' work, *The Hidden Lincoln,* Viking Press, p. 371–73.) Benjamin Vineyard accompanied his letter to Jesse Weik (March 14, 1887) with the following account:

Mary S. Owens, daughter of Nathaniel Owens, was born in Green County, Kentucky, on the 29th day of September, 1808. She was married to Jesse Vineyard on the 27th day of March, 1841. Of this union there were born five children, of whom only two survive. Jesse Vineyard died December 27th, 1862, and Mary, his widow, on July 4th, 1877.

Mary received a good education, her father being a leading and wealthy citizen of his time and locality. A part of her schooling was obtained in a Catholic convent, though in religous faith she was a Baptist, and in after years united with that denomination, and continued a member thereof until the time of her death. She was good looking when a girl, by many esteemed handsome, but growing fleshier as she grew older. She was polished in her manners, pleasing in her address and attractive in society. She had a little dash of coquetry in her intercourse with that class of young men, who arrogated to themselves claims of superiority. But she never yielded to this disposition to an extent that would willingly lend encouragement to an honest suitor, sincerely desirous of securing her hand, where she felt she could not in the end yield to a proposal of marriage if he should make the offer. She was a good conversationalist and a splendid reader—but very few persons being found to equal her in this accomplishment. She was light-hearted and cheery in her disposition. She was kind and considerate for those, with whom she was thrown in contact.

She first became acquainted with Mr. Lincoln while visiting a sister of hers who had married Bennett Able, and who was an early settler of the Country about New Salem. Young Lincoln was a frequent visitor at the house of Able and a warm friend of the family, and during the first visit of Mary Owens, which did not continue a great while, he learned to admire her very much. Later she made a second visit to her sister, Mrs. Able, returning with her from Kentucky. Lincoln had boasted, so it has been said, that he would marry Miss Owens if she came a second time to Illinois, a report of which had come to her hearing. She left her Kentucky home with a predetermination to show him, if she met him, that she was not to be caught simply by the asking. On this second visit Lincoln paid her more marked attention than ever before, and his affections became more and more enlisted in her behalf. During the early part of their acquaintance, following the natural bent of her temperament, she was pleasing and entertaining to him. Later on he discovered himself seriously interested in the blue-eyed Kentuckian, whom he had really under-estimated in his preconceived opinions of her. In the meantime, Mary, too, had discovered the sterling qualities of the young man, who was paying her such devoted attention. But while she admired, she did not love him. He was ungainly and angular in his physical make-up, and to her seemed deficient in the nicer and more delicate attentions, which she felt to be due from the man whom she had pictured as an ideal husband. He had given her to understand that she had greatly charmed him. But he was not himself certain that he could make her the husband he thought she would be most happy with. Later on, by word and in letter he told her so. His honesty of purpose showed itself in all his efforts to win her hand. He told her of his poverty, and while advising her that life with him meant to her, who had been reared in comfort and plenty, great privation and sacrifice, yet he wished to secure her as a wife. But she felt that she did not entertain for him the same feeling that he professed for her, and that she ought to entertain before accepting him, and so declined his offer. Judging alone from some of his letters it has been supposed by some that she, remembering the rumor she had heard of his determination to marry her, and not being fully certain of the sincerity of his purposes, may have purposely left him, in the earlier stages of his courtship somewhat in uncertainty. But later on, when, by his manner and his repeated announcement to her that his hand and heart were at her disposal, he demonstrated the honesty and sincerity of his purposes, she declined his offer kindly but with no uncertain meaning. In speaking of him in after years she always referred to him as a man with a heart full of human kindness and a head full of common sense.

Weik was so pleased with the son's characterization of his mother in regard to her "coquetry" that he interpolated verbatim, without quotation marks, a portion of Vineyard's manuscript into the Herndon-Weik biography.

In regard to the account of the romance, as well as the photograph, Vineyard wrote Weik the following letter, a photostat of which is now in the collection of the Department of Lincolniana at Lincoln Memorial University, Harrogate, Tennessee:

ST. JOSEPH, MO., March 14, 1887

MR. JESSE W. WEIK,
GREEN CASTLE, IND.

Dear Sir,—I have just returned from my sisters near Weston and gotten from her to send you the ambrotype of my mother taken many years before the photograph a copy of which I sent you. The photograph was taken when she was about sixty-five—the ambrotype was taken perhaps twenty-five or thirty years earlier. I had forgotten that this old picture existed, until seeing my sister it was brought to my recollection. We do not know the date when the ambrotype was taken but we think it was probably taken when she was about the age of thirty-five. I run the risk of sending you this ambrotype of my mother by this day's express. Please let me know as soon as you get it, and return it to me as soon as through using it. By taking in a reprint—the face and bust only for the benefit of your readers I am sure that it will be much more satisfactory than the photograph I sent you before.

I see the fashion was for the ladies to wear caps those days, and by suggesting the reprint of the face and bust only, I do not mean that you should exclude the cap if you think it should appear as is probably the case.

I send you also inclosed the original letter of Mr. Lincoln to my mother dated August 16th, 1837, which I got from my sister. Please take the best of care of it, and return it to me by mail just as soon as you can get through using it. You see I am trusting you (a stranger) considerably. I trust my confidence will not be misplaced.

I have written (also inclosed) a short account of my mother and Mr. Lincoln's courtship of her. I do not wish it published over my signature, but send it to you as my idea of what is probably true, that it may serve you as the basis of what you may wish to write on the subject.

Please acknowledge receipt of this, as soon as it reaches you.

I received your last with contents as stated.

Yours truly,
B. R. VINEYARD

In January and February, 1887, B. R. Vineyard wrote again

215

to Jesse Weik concerning his mother and Lincoln's offer of marriage. Nancy G. Vineyard, a half-sister of Mary Owens, also wrote Weik from Victoria, Texas, on February 4, 1887, relating facts concerning the courtship of her sister and Lincoln. References to these letters appear in an index to the Weik manuscripts, but after an exhaustive search they have not been discovered.

Lincoln collectors will be interested in learning that all three of Lincoln's letters to Mary Owens are extant. They were carefully preserved by Mrs. Vineyard during her lifetime in the drawer of an old bureau in a farmhouse near Weston, Missouri. When she died the letters were lost for a while, as they had been removed from their hiding-place. Mrs. Charles L. Barbee, of Kansas City, Missouri, an adopted daughter of Mrs. Kate Cunningham, discovered them stuffed in the rafters of the old home place. She realized their value and importance and carefully preserved them. Mrs. Cunningham, a daughter of Mary Owens, inherited the three letters. She distributed them among certain members of the family, with the request that they be handed down from generation to generation.

The Lincoln letter dated December 13, 1836, is today in the possession of a great-grandson, James G. Vineyard, 1128 Dierks Building, Kansas City, Missouri. The one dated May 7, 1837, is the property of Mrs. George H. Vineyard, 819 Felix Street, St. Joseph, Missouri, the widow of a grandson. The August 16, 1837, letter is said to be in the possession of Miss Lena Parrott, of Augusta, Maine. Her grandmother was a half-sister of Mary Owens. Members of the family have received fabulous offers for the letters (one account states they were offered $30,000 for the three items), but the letters are not for sale. However, photostats of the originals may be had from the larger Lincoln libraries.

In the year 1869, Herndon turned over to Ward H. Lamon copies of his Lincoln letters and documents for publication in Lamon's biography, *The Life of Abraham Lincoln* (James R. Osgood and Company, Boston, 1872). In this great mass of data Lamon found considerable information on the courtship of Lincoln and Mary Owens, but not being satisfied as to its completeness, he made an investigation for additional material and was amply rewarded for his trouble. Lamon, with an eye and ear for new facts concerning Lincoln, remembered hearing some time during the Lincoln administration that Mrs. Orville H. Browning, wife of the Illinois senator, had received from Lincoln an interesting letter dated April 1, 1838, about a romance, and upon inquiry he was not only allowed to see the original letter, but to make a copy. Putting two and two together, he found this letter was a sequel to the Lincoln-Owens romance, written in the same month that Miss Owens made her final departure from Illinois. Knowing that this letter would be a bombshell in historical circles, he gave a long explanation as to why he had determined that it should be published. He wrote, on pages 180–81 of his biography:

> For many reasons the publication of this letter is an extremely painful duty. If it could be withheld, and the act decently reconciled to the conscience of a biographer professing to be honest and candid, it should never see the light in these pages. Its grotesque humor, its coarse exaggerations in describing the person of a lady whom the writer was willing to marry, its imputation of toothless

and weather-beaten old age to a woman really young and handsome, its utter lack of that delicacy of tone and sentiment which one naturally expects a gentleman to adopt when he thinks proper to discuss the merits of his late mistress,—all these, and its defective orthography, it would certainly be more agreeable to suppress than to publish. But, if we begin by omitting or mutilating a document which sheds so broad a light upon one part of his life and one phase of his character, why may we not do the like as fast and as often as the temptations arise? and where shall the process cease? A biography worth writing at all is worth writing fully and honestly; and the writer who suppresses or mangles the truth is no better than he who bears false witness in any other capacity.

Accordingly, Lamon published Lincoln's letter to Mrs. Browning:

SPRINGFIELD, April 1, 1838

DEAR MADAM:

Without appologising for being egotistical, I shall make the history of so much of my own life, as has elapsed since I saw you, the subject of this letter—And by the way I now discover, that, in order to give a full and inteligible account of the things I have done and suffered *since* I saw you, I shall necessarily have to relate some that happened *before*—

It was, then, in the autumn of 1836, that a married lady of my acquaintance, and who was a great friend of mine, being about to pay a visit to her father and other relatives residing in Kentucky, proposed to me, that on her return she would bring a sister of hers with her, upon condition that I would engage to become her brother-in-law with all convenient dispach—I, of course, accepted the proposal; for you know I could not have done otherwise, had I really been averse to it; but privately between you and me, I was most confoundedly well pleased with the project—I had seen the said sister some three years before, thought her inteligent and agreeable, and saw no good objection to plodding life through hand in hand with her—Time passed on, the lady took her journey and in due time returned, sister in company sure enough—This stomached me a little;

for it appeared to me, that her coming so readily showed that she was a trifle too willing; but on reflection it occurred to me, that she might have been prevailed on by her married sister to come, without any thing concerning me ever having been mentioned to her; and so I concluded that if no other objection presented itself, I would consent to wave this—All this occurred upon my *hearing* of her arrival in the neighborhood; for, be it remembered, I had not yet *seen* her, except about three years previous, as before mentioned—

In a few days we had an interview, and although I had seen her before, she did not look as my imagination had pictured her—I knew she was over-size, but she now appeared a fair match for Falstaff; I knew she was called an "old maid," and I felt no doubt of the truth of at least half of the appelation; but now, when I beheld her, I could not for my life avoid thinking of my mother; and this, not from withered features, for her skin was too full of fat, to permit its contracting in to wrinkles; but from her want of teeth, weather-beaten appearance in general, and from a kind of notion that ran in my head that *nothing* could have commenced at the size of infancy, and reached her present bulk in less than thirty-five or forty years; and, in short, I was not all pleased with her—But what could I do? I had told her sister that I would take her for better or for worse; and I made a point of honor and conscience in all things, to stick to my word, especially if others had been induced to act on it, which in this case I doubted not they had, for I was now fairly convinced, that no other man on earth would have her, and hence the conclusion that they were bent on holding me to my bargain—Well, thought I, I have said it, and, be consequences what they may, it shall not be my fault if I fail to do it—At once I determined to consider her my wife; and this done, all my powers of discovery were put to the rack, in search of perfections in her, which might be fairly set-off, against her defects—I tried to imagine she was handsome, which, but for her unfortunate corpulency, was actually true—Exclusive of this, no woman that I have seen, has a finer face—I also tried to convince myself, that the mind was much more to be valued than the person; and in this, she was not inferior, as I could discover, to any with whom I had been acquainted—

Shortly after this, without attempting to come to any positive understanding with her, I set out for Vandalia, where and when you first saw me—During my stay there, I had letters from her, which did not change my opinion of either her intellect or intention; but on the contrary, confirmed it in both—

All this while, although I was fixed "firm as the surge repelling rock" in my resolution, I found I was continually repenting the rashness, which had led me to make it—Through life I have been in no bondage, either real or imaginary from the thraldom of which I so much desired to be free—

After my return home, I saw nothing to change my opinion of her in any particular—She was the same and so was I—I now spent my time between planning how I might get along through life after my contemplated change of circumstances should have taken place; and how I might procrastinate the evil day for a time, which I really dreaded as much—perhaps more, than an irishman does the halter—

After all my suffering upon this deeply interesting subject, here I am, wholly, unexpectedly, completely out of the "scrape"; and I now want to know, if you can guess how I got out of it—Out clear in every sense of the term; no violation of word, honor, or conscience—I don't believe you can guess, and so I may as well tell you at once—As the lawyers say, it was done in the manner following towit—After I had delayed the matter as long as I thought I could in honor do, which by the way had brought me round into the last fall, I concluded I might as well bring it to a consumation without further delay; and so I mustered my resolution, and made the proposal to her direct; but, shocking to relate, she answered, No—At first I supposed she did it through an affectation of modesty, which I thought but ill became her, under the peculiar circumstances of her case; but on my renewal of the charge, I found she repeled it with greater firmness than before—I tried it again and again, but with the same success, or rather with the same want of success—I finally was forced to give it up, at which I very unexpectedly found myself mortified almost beyond endurance—I was mortified, it seemed to me, in a hundred different ways—My vanity was deeply wounded by the reflection, that I had so long been too stupid to discover her intentions, and at the same time never doubting that I understood them perfectly; and also, that she whom I had taught myself to believe no body else would have, had actually rejected me with all my fancied greatness; and to cap the whole, I then, for the first time, began to suspect that I was really a little in love with her—But let it all go—I'll try and outlive it—Others have been made fools of by the girls; but this can never be with truth said of me—I most emphatically, in this instance, made a fool of myself—I have now come to the conclusion never again to think of marrying, and for this reason; I can never be satisfied with anyone who would be block-head enough to have me—

When you receive this, write me a long yarn about something to amuse me—Give my respects to Mr. Browning—

Your sincere friend
A. LINCOLN

MRS. O. H. BROWNING—

True to Lamon's expectations, adverse comments were bantered about over his indiscretions. Two interesting letters, now the property of the Chicago Historical Society, reveal caustic criticisms and lengthy explanations of the April Fool's Day missive.

In a letter from Chicago dated November 22, 1872, and written by Isaac N. Arnold to O. H. Browning, one reads the following remarks:

Most of his [Lamon's] book, it seems to me is filled up with trivial and insignificant matters which only prurient curiosity would care for and without any apprecation of the noblest traits of his character. I have just been reading a letter to Mrs. Browning (pages 181–182) which he says it was an "extremely painful duty to publish." If the letter is genuine I cannot conceive the motives which made it his duty to publish it. If you feel at liberty to tell me, I should be very glad to know the history of this letter.

Accordingly O. H. Browning, on November 25, 1872, wrote Isaac N. Arnold from Quincy, Illinois. In regard to the letter he made the following statement:

The letter published in the biography, purporting to have been written to Mrs. Browning, is genuine. In the winter of 1836–7 we were all at Vandalia, then the seat of government of the state. I was a member of the Senate and Mr. Lincoln of the House of Representatives. He and I had been previously acquainted, but he then first made the acquaintance of Mrs. Browning. We all boarded at the same house. He was very fond of Mrs. Browning's society, and spent many of his evenings and much of his leisure time, at our rooms. We were all there together again in the winter of 1837–8, the same relations subsisting between us as during the preceding winter. After our return home, in the spring of 1838 the letter in question was received. We were very much amused with it, but Mrs. Browning and myself supposed it to be a fiction; a creation of his brain; one of his funny stories, without any foundation of fact to sustain it. It was laid away, among other letters, and forgotten. In 1861 I was overhauling a correspondence which had been accumulating for years and destroying many hundreds of letters which I regarded as no longer of any value. This with other letters of Mr. Lincoln's was then exhumed, and saved from the common fate, only because it was amusing and written a long time ago, in the very characteristic style of the then President.

We permitted a few of our friends, both here and at Washington, to see it, merely as a matter of curiosity and amusement; we still laboring under the impression that it was pure romance.

I think it was in 1862 that a gentleman who was collecting materials for a biography of Mr. Lincoln, having heard of this letter, called on Mrs. Browning in the city and requested a copy. She declined to give it. The first time she was at the President's, only a few days after, she informed him of the request that had been made and asked him what he had to say in regard to it. She then first learned from him that the narrative of the letter was not fiction but a true account of an incident in actual life. He added that others of the actors than himself were still living; that it might be painful to them to see the letter in print; and that on their account he desired it should be withheld for the present; but that hereafter, when those most interested should have passed away, she might exercise her own discretion. After the death of Mr. Lincoln one of his most intimate friends, Col. Lamon, who was on confidential relations with the President through the entire period of his administration, was permitted at his earnest request, to take a copy; but upon the distinct understanding that it should never be used in connection with Mrs. Browning's name. I do not see how Mr. Lincoln can justly be censured for writing the letter. It was written in the confidence of friendship, with no purpose, or expectation, that it would ever become public. No names were mentioned, nor was it likely that any other name than his own would ever be known in connection with it. His only object seemed to be to amuse a friend at his own expense.

No injury was done to anyone by the mere writing of the letter, nor would there have been in its publication, unaccompanied by the explanation given by his biographer; and for these Mr. Lincoln ought not to be held responsible.

Neither Mrs. Browning nor myself ever knew from him who the lady referred to in the letter was. Of course neither of us ever asked him, nor did he ever inform us. If the feelings of others have been injured, I think it is chargeable upon the biographer, and not upon Mr. Lincoln.

The Arnold-Browning correspondence in its complete form may be found in the Barker pamphlet, *Abraham Lincoln and Mary Owen,* privately printed. The late Mr. Harry Barker, of Los Angeles, who had formerly lived at Springfield, Illinois, at one time purchased the Lincoln-Browning letter, along with the letters of Arnold and Browning. In a letter dated August 2, 1940, he stated that they had been acquired from a Mrs. Price, a niece of the Brownings, who had inherited them. He sold them for $535.00 to Major Lambert, and of that amount, $500.00 was for the Lincoln letter. The letter written by Lincoln to Mrs. Browning is on letter-size paper, covering both sides of two sheets, and one side of a third. At the sale of Lambert's collection in 1914, the letter was bid in for $1250.00 by George D. Smith, and was passed on by him to the Henry E. Huntington Library. Morris H. Briggs, in his article, "Lincoln Autograph Material," in the

February 16, 1929, issue of *Publisher's Weekly*, stated that the Lincoln-Browning letter sold for $1,250.00, but in 1929 would sell for over $17,000.00.

When Lamon and subsequent biographers of Lincoln published the Lincoln-Browning letter they failed to decipher it correctly. In the second paragraph Lincoln wrote: "This stomached me a little. . . . . ." The word "stomached" was misread by Lamon and printed in his book "astonished." While the letter was in the possession of Mr. Barker he noted the mistake, and both Carl Sandburg and William E. Barton accepted the correction.

When Nicolay and Hay published their serial in the *Century Magazine* entitled: "Abraham Lincoln: A History," they discussed the Lincoln-Owens courtship, and of course mentioned the Lincoln-Browning letter. Their explanation of it was the same as that advanced by Browning. The third instalment, which was published in January, 1887, led to an interesting, if not critical, correspondence between Milton Hay, of Springfield, and his nephew, John Hay, the author-statesman. Among other things, Milton wrote:

I confess the Browning letter—the circumstance that it was written at all by Mr. Lincoln and to a woman—that this woman, a professed friend, should have carefully preserved it and have given it out to a publisher (another dear friend) for publication and by him published to the world, are enigmas to me and probably will remain so, as I doubt very much whether your explanation, explains. . . . .

This letter in its entirety has been published in *Bulletin No. 25* of The Abraham Lincoln Association (December 1931, p. 6–9).

Herndon's reactions to the Lincoln-Browning letter are contained in his unpublished article entitled, "Lincoln's Courtship with Miss Owens." He made the following comments: "Miss Owens rejected Mr. Lincoln's hand, and returned to Kentucky in '38. Mr. Lincoln was elected to the legislature in '38. From Vandalia Mr. Lincoln wrote a letter to Mrs. O. H. Browning—the wife of Hon. O. H. Browning another member of the legislature, dated April 1st, '38. In this letter Lincoln described Miss Owens most graphically from then [?] standpoint: it is a curious letter and one that deserves to be read and studied with care in connection with the above letters of Mr. Lincoln to Miss Owens. One question the very first question that comes up and demands solution in the mind of the reader is this—was Mr. Lincoln in love with Miss Owens? The second question is this, did Mr. Lincoln speak truly when he wrote his letters to her or did he wish to back down, drive the woman off through fear of his want of a real attachment, as appears in his letters.

"Miss Owens rejected Mr. Lincoln's hand because she saw in him a deficiency of those little links which make up the chain of woman's happiness—at least it was so in her case. Shrewd woman—intuitive [?] woman—wise woman."

The above paragraph is crossed out in the manuscript. Along the left margin of the page is a note so heavily crossed out as to be in part almost indecipherable. So far as it can be deciphered, it reads: "I have seen [?] the [?] [?] that a historian [?] applied to Mr. Lincoln and he said it was too true [?]."

Herndon digressed a little in regard to the true feeling of Lincoln for Miss Owens by stating: "Miss Owens herself—

her bright and highly esteemed son B. R. Vineyard of Missouri—an excellent lawyer and a gentleman—Mrs. Bennett Able and all the relatives of the family, do acknowledge that the letters written by Lincoln to Miss Owens was sincerely—truthfully—honestly written and so acted on them. All persons who knew Mr. Lincoln, when living and now when dead believe, that the letters expressed his honest feelings and his deepest convictions [?] and that they were written sincerely—truthfully and honestly and I do [?] believe what all others believe who knew Lincoln well. Mr. Lincoln was a very conscientious man—a man of fine feelings—an honest man—a man of the very highest human integrity. Lincoln was all this and more than this, but the letter must be explained: It will not do to say—it's not so. It will take some argument to explain it and I shall proceed to explain it in my way."

Like Milton Hay of Springfield, Herndon did not approve of the way in which Nicolay and Hay in the January, 1887, number of the *Century* attempted to explain the Lincoln-Browning letter. In making his explanation Herndon wrote: "Messrs. Nicolay & Hay say in the Jany. number of the Century for 1887 at pages 379–80 this—among other things, about Lincoln, Miss Owens, Mrs. Browning and the letter which Lincoln wrote to Mrs. Browning—'This letter (the one dated the April the 1st 1838 and written by Mr. Lincoln from Vandalia to Mrs. O. H. Browning—When Mrs. Browning having been asked to furnish it to a biographer—she was warned against doing so by the President himself, who said there was too much truth in it for print.' Some historian or biographer doubtless applied to her for a copy of the letter for publication, and it is true that Mrs. Browning refused to give a copy of the letter until she wrote to Mr. Lincoln or otherwise ascertained his wish and gave his consent to its publication and it was at this request that Mr. Lincoln as suppose(d) refused his consent to the publication of the letter. This letter was a private letter addressed to a lady. Now there are some serious questions to answer. First—did Mr. (L.) say what is told by Nicolay & Hay; and secondly if so what were the conditions of Lincoln and what were his motives. In the first place I do not believe that Lincoln ever said what he is made to say in the Century and I never shall believe it till I see some gentleman of undoubted veracity, who will, on his honor say that what Mr. Lincoln is supposed to have said was said in fact. Lincoln was a gentleman of great sincerity— brimfull of truth—a man of the greatest integrity—a man who would be sacrificed before he would play [?] the false to a woman's deep and profoundest love. This man's heart was too good and his general [?] nature too noble to play hypocrite with a woman's love. What—this great noble man play with a woman's love and deepest and warmest affections that he might watch and weigh her sufferings! Never."

Continuing his discussion Herndon said: "Supposing however, that such a conscientious—honest and truthful man were to come and say to me 'I heard Mr. Lincoln say what I make him say' I might believe it. I should have to weigh Lincoln—the asserted fact and the gentleman's honor, but suppose I believed the man—then what? I would know that the letter was written in '38 and I would suppose that what Lincoln said—or is made to say happened or took place while

Lincoln was President and in '61 or after that time. From the date of the letter in '38 to '61 there would have passed some 23 years—23 years of Mr. Lincoln's most busy—most active—most ambitious—most anxious and most harassing, if not most miserable life. I should suppose that he had forgotten the whole contents of the letter—their full import and intent [?]. This is I honestly believe due to Mr. Lincoln; and if I were driven from this position I should say that Lincoln got into one of those overwhelming and irresistible states of humor—fun—one of those jolly humorous states, tinged with sadness, he being lonesome and had nothing to say but be humorous, that he wrote the unfortunate letter, in the inspiration of the moment and if I were driven from this position I should say and say it by way of confession and avoidance as I have said, it may be a hundred times, that Mr. Lincoln had not a quick perception of the propriety of things; nor did Mr. Lincoln have a good judgment of quick passing things. Mr. Lincoln to have profound judgments must have his time to think and if he had not time to think his judgments were poor indeed, and from this position I never can be driven."

Ending his explanation of the Lincoln-Browning letter, to Weik, Herndon wrote: "Miss Owens rejected Lincoln's hand, because she saw in him and only that, to his discredit as lover and husband the full deficiency of those little attributes and links which go to make up the full chain of woman's happiness—at least this deficiency in Lincoln was seen by her fully—quickly and accurately. Shrewd woman—intuitive woman—sharp wise woman!"

Students and readers who have probed into Lincoln's life, deeds and character, and have studied his addresses, speeches, and letters, have come to the conclusion that Lincoln violated no code of honor, that he was guilty of no improprieties, and that he wrote the letter to Mrs. Browning on April Fool's Day in the spirit of levity. He meant no offense, he mentioned no names, he never intended the letter for the eyes of the public. Why should we not then accept the letter as a contribution to the wit and humor of Abraham Lincoln?

Printed in the United States
145716LV00002B/91/A

9 781406 731101